Sacred
UNIONS,
Sacred
PASSIONS

DAN BRENNAN

Sacred
UNIONS,
Sacred
PASSIONS

Engaging the Mystery of Friendship Between
Men and Women

Faith Dance Publishing

Elgin, Illinois

Faith Dance Publishing

Elgin, Illinois

Sacred Unions, Sacred Passions

© 2010 Dan Brennan

Requests for information should be sent to:

www.sacredunionssacredpassions.com

Library of Congress Cataloging-in-Publication Data

Brennan, Dan

Sacred Unions, Sacred Passions : Engaging the Mystery of Friendship Between Men and Women

ISBN   978-0-9825807-0-7 (softcover)

1. Religion 2. Spirituality

Cover and interior design by Sue Mihalovic, Bramblewoods

Printed in the United States of America.

To my own best friend, my wife Sheila,
who embraces the beauty, goodness, and truth of friendship
with all the passion of her being.

CONTENTS

Sacred Unions, Sacred Passions

FOREWORD

Methinks that friendship has fallen on hard times. When Facebook announces that a subscriber has "469 friends" I have to wonder what "friend" has come to mean in today's parlance.

While the concept of friendship has been expanded to such a degree that it has largely been diluted, the concept of intimacy has been narrowed to mean primarily sexual intimacy, and, within the Christian community, exclusively marital sexual intimacy.

Daniel's book attempts to recapture a deeper (and thereby narrower) understanding of friendship and a wider understanding of intimacy within spiritual friendship. Although his focus is friendship between the sexes, much of what I read here is apropos of deeply intimate, committed friendship—period.

My comments—unlike Dan's—are not rooted in years of reading and studying but simply in my many miles on the road of life tasting the good gifts of our gracious God along the way.

As Dan and I have grown in God's friendship with us and our friendship with one another, we've come to cherish increasingly those very special additional friendships with which God has blessed us on this journey.

I am a mathematician. Because my choice of vocation was made prior to the influx of women into this field, my significant friendships were necessarily formed with men, men who shared my field of study and work. At the time, I didn't think, "Wow, I have cross-gender friendships here!" They were friendships with all the richness that the word implied and without any additional modifiers or surgeon-general warnings.

In that mix were a few particularly close relationships. My best friend during my graduate school years was a married man. Our paths diverged many years ago (and not in "a yellow wood"), but his lifeprints shaped me as a person and as a professional. I love him still and always will.

How in the world can a married man and a single woman have a close, chaste friendship? Back then it was a "no brainer" for both of us. Our mutual love and respect established our parameters from Day One. But those parameters did not shut out love or companionship or soul-sharing. Precisely because we made choices (unspoken) to honor his marriage and one another, our friendship thrived in the midst of the steamy sexual revolution that was tearing through campus. No conferences or seminars or counseling were necessary during that time. We knew who we were and what we were about. Additionally, no one within our social context regarded such friendships as dangerous or undesirable.

The female friends that Dan counts as his closest are my friends, too! Indeed, they do not reside *outside* our marriage or *alongside* our marriage but *inside* our marriage. If we've learned anything about loving during these twenty-eight years of marriage, it is that with God as the true source of love, we have an infinitely abundant source! Loving is not a zero-sum game.

Friendship love is one of God's sweet gifts for our earthly pilgrimage, one gift that we can take with us into eternity. There is chemistry here, of a kind. There is mystery here. Take off your shoes because this is holy ground! The Lord God himself visits us embodied in a friend. Friendship is incarnational.

When our son, Jonathan, was quite young and fearful of the dark, we explained Psalm 139, declaring that God was right there in the room with him, that it was never dark for God. Jonathan did not dispute any of these foundational truths, but he passionately cried out, "I want someone with bones in them!"

When the Lord gives us a friend, he himself comes to us "with bones."

The scholarly and sublime treasure that is this book is the fruit of many years of experiencing cross-gender friendships and meditating upon their beauty and blessing. Wishing to share this world of wonder with a church often locked in fear and distrust, Dan presents a "thick" understanding of scriptural passages, an accumulation of historical testimony from inside and outside the Church, and a complete discussion of contemporary thinkers on this subject.

It is our prayer that this book will call the Church toward greater reconciliation between men and women, greater freedom to love one another with that very love with which we ourselves have been loved from the foundations of the world, a deeper experience of "God with us."

Thy kingdom come;
thy will be done on earth
as it is in heaven.
Amen.

Sheila Wilson Brennan
October 2009

Sacred Unions, Sacred Passions

ACKNOWLEDGEMENTS

A book like this would have never happened were it not for friends who believed in the virtue and beauty of friendship between the sexes. I owe a great debt to the community of friends who encouraged me when I began to dream about this book on my blog. They include Katherine Becker, Dana Ames, Maria Henderson, Kevin Corcoran, and Sue Schick. Your faithful support and prayers from the beginning until now have been a constant reminder of God's personal goodness to me in this wild and sometimes unpredictable adventure. Your presence may not be readily visible in the book but the Lord knows what you have meant to me in this journey.

I owe another level of special thanks to those friends who came on after the beginning but who became strong supporters and friends. To Mike Morrell, you will never know how your first email inspired me with fresh hope that this book was needed in the Christian community. I am deeply grateful for your passion to see this happen and for all you have done to facilitate that. To Christa Miller, your friendship has blessed me and has touched me. To Maria Kirby, thank you for your rich support and prayers. To Stephanie Pavlakis Britcher, your testimony of flourishing shalom inspires me to believe that others who read this book may find help. To Barbara and Darren Miller, your enthusiastic online presence deserves special mention - thank you. To Kathy Escobar, your authentic posts were extraordinary encouragement. To Sue Mihalovic, thank you for pouring your creative gifts and energy into the interior and exterior design. I am indebted to your beautiful and generous contribution in seeing the manuscript become a book.

I owe a special debt to those men and women who have gone before me and paved the way for me to even consider going deeper in my own friendships with women: Jack Balswick, Judith Balswick, Wendy M.

Wright, Dennis Hiebert, Lisa Gee, Kathy Werking, Michael Monsour, William Rawlins, Lisa Graham McMinn, Jane Tibbetts Schulenburg, Edith Humphrey, and Carole Hallundbaek.

To Susan Matheson, your strong encouragement expressed in so many ways during this season has been one of God's greatest gifts to me. I did not consistently heed your plea for shorter chapters, but I am thankful for your belief in me and my ability to write this. I wished we lived closer to each other.

I am very thankful to Susanne Osborne. Even though you were not around at the start, you entered into the dance of friendship, and I have been richly blessed as you have poured beauty and goodness into me as we have prayed together and dialogued. As a single woman, you have not been afraid to express delight in me, and that is so refreshing and uplifting. You know how to enter into delight and celebration in the moment, and you know how to hear pain. It is not a common thing to see delight expressed between a married man and single woman in the evangelical community, but may this book encourage more delight in similar friendships! You may have come onto the scene only in the past year, but our dance has become so precious.

To Jennifer Roach, I cannot adequately describe your beauty in our friendship. You have given so much support. You have truly opened your heart wide and have celebrated all my small victories in this journey, but you have also been there for me during the valleys of my greatest doubts. You, too, have not held back your delight in me, and in this book. You know the language of delight and beauty in friendship and you have been so generous. I have appreciated how our friendship has grown. I am a much better man because of your unique beauty, presence, and voice in my life. Thank you for your trust in me, your belief in me, and your tender transparency for so many years. Without your support, I would not be here.

To Jennifer Ould, you are another irreplaceable friend in the journey to write this book. Would there even be a book without your unique beauty and presence in my life? While God has brought you to embrace male-female friendships through your own story with your own convictions, our esteem for each other is greater than our differences. Your distinctive presence and leadership have shaped every page of this book. You have taught me to love those who disagree with me, to see the best in those who have opposed me. When I had my deepest doubts, you would not let me give up hope. You have prayed big prayers for me on days when I have been my weakest. I am a better man and husband because of our confessional friendship and your fierce love for Sheila. I am truly blessed to know you as a sister in Christ.

To all who have generously volunteered their time, energy, and input into reading and editing either some or all of my drafts: Jonathan Brennan, Katherine Becker, Sue Schick, Susan Matheson, Dana Ames, Kevin Corcoran, Lilian Calles Barger, Michael Morrell, Liz Carmichael, Edith Humphrey, Susanne Osborne, Jennifer Roach, Jennifer Ould, Jack Balswick, Father John Fortin, Jenell Paris, Carole Hallundbaek, and last but not least, Sheila, my beloved wife. Whatever mistakes are in the book are mine. I so thank you for the gifts of time and insight you shared with me.

To those I haven't mentioned, because for various reasons, I cannot or must not, I thank you. Due to the present cultural climate in the evangelical community, there are friends who should be but cannot be acknowledged because of the repercussions. I know pastors who have close friendships with individuals from the other sex but are clearly fearful of that becoming known and misunderstood. For singles who enjoy such friendships, but who are fearful that their romantic opportunities would be jeopardized, I thank you all. I sincerely thank those who have differed with me, who have pushed me to think about this complex subject even more deeply.

And my greatest thanks to Sheila. What a wild journey this has been! I treasure your beauty more than ever. You have not only had to endure my nights and days of writing but also many discouragements along the way. The road has been hard and glorious. I so delight in your companionship. You believed in me from day one, and you have not wavered. A whole new world was opened to us when we came to see that married life in the kingdom is not a zero sum game of intimacy.

INTRODUCTION

What would our marriages, our friendships, our churches, and our communities look like if men and women were not afraid of connecting with each other in deep ways? What if men and women could really know each other without sex getting in the way? What if we did not have to be so afraid of our own and other's bodies that we cannot trust ourselves with them?

These are important questions for Christian men and women who are integrating new meaning and depth in marriage and friendship in our postmodern world. Sweeping social changes in our understanding of masculinity, femininity, marriage, friendship, community, family, and spirituality in the West are changing the ways men and women relate to each other as spouses, co-workers, and friends. Thousands of men and women are working together, flying together as co-workers, and commuting together—all without "chaperones." They are now working in close proximity alongside each other in ministries. Friendships between the sexes are increasing in contemporary culture and, even more significantly, transmarital friendship love is emerging as a sacred option for husbands and wives in Christ-honoring marriages. More than ever, friendship love between a man and woman is poised to become a receptive love coexisting *with* marriage not a rival love *to* it.

This book makes a simple but provocative claim: stories of paired cross-sex friendship love are journeys toward communion with God and our neighbor in the Christian story. In the new creation, men and women are not limited to stark contrasts where we must choose between romantic passion in marriage or inappropriate sex/infidelity. Chaste, but powerfully close friendships between the sexes stir our curiosity and resist formulaic gender roles in marriage, friendship, and society. In the Christian story, men and women were made for each other—and they are called into the communion of love. And while there is a distinctive calling for supreme allegiance and communion in marriage, the way of friendship between the sexes is the quest for beauty, goodness, and truth in marriage, in relationships extending outward from marriage (from here on referred to as "transmarital," thank you, Marva Dawn!) or outside marriage if one is single. Communion between sexes is not *solely* contained between husband and wife.

I do not offer a particular model for this sacred friendship in the following pages. Interpersonal communion cannot be reduced to one model. Nor does the Christian community need more how-to books on male-female relations. I have tasted some of the beauty and sweetness of female friendships—beginning with my wife, Sheila. I have not arrived on any perfectionist plateau. I am a flawed friend as those closest to me know. I do acknowledge Dan Allender's counsel and confess how much of a mess I am.[1] My closest friends know I do not have it all together. I own my struggles in my friendships. The formation and nurturance of intimate relationships is never an easy stroll along a sun-drenched beach. Part of the spiritual formation in friendship is working through disconnects, hurts, misunderstandings, and honest mistakes. I would like to think, though, that I am maturing in these relationships and have a growing sense of learning from my failures. To my amazement, my dearest female friends know me very deeply, yet they have stuck around, and I am a better man because of their distinctive and unique beauty.

It is not my intention to romanticize cross-sex friendship. We will not get very far in sexual formation and virtue if we approach this relationship with rose-colored glasses. No friendship starts out with perfect people. On this side of heaven, there will never be a friendship between a man and a woman who have arrived and have male-female relations all figured out for everyone else. This is not a book about ten steps to cross-sex friendship perfection. No single book can possibly address the wide-ranging issues impacting friendships between the sexes. Although plenty of books on marriage are published every year, the Christian community has yet to seriously engage the richness of male-female friendship and sexuality. It is undeniably true that many evangelical leaders tend to see deep male-female friendships as a threat to marriage.

This book suggests that the possibility of deep spiritual friendships between the sexes may decrease the divorce rate among Christians. I don't disagree with the plight of marriages. Instead of reinforcing outdated stereotypes of masculinity and femininity accompanied by overromanticized views of marriage, the Christian community ought to reconsider the practice of spiritual friendship where men and women are co-creators, co-equal, and co-commissioned to advance God's beauty, goodness, peace, and justice in this world. Many deep spiritual friendships between men and women in church history lasted longer than some contemporary Christian marriages.

I ask for your patience as I have had to make specific choices about language concerning this type of relationship. What to call them? Male-female friendships? Cross-sex? Cross-gender? Opposite-sex? All of these have their own strengths and weaknesses. There are purists who stick with one or the other. I primarily stay with the phrase "cross-sex friendships." When I am addressing relationships where both the man and woman are committed to chastity within their friendship but are open to intimacy, I did not want to use the word "nonsexual." It is impossible for them to be "nonsexual" in their intimacy. They are both embodied sexual beings. People cannot leave their sexuality at the door when they enter friendship with persons of the other gender. Embracing a healthy, positive, chaste view of one's sexuality in friendship is an expression of beauty, goodness, and truth in God's story. So, I mostly choose to use the phrase "nonromantic" to describe close male-female relationships signifying romantic love and sex are off-limits.

Centuries before the contemporary distinction of sex and sexuality, Christian men and women formed deep friendships of mutual love, delight, acceptance, affection, confession, prayer, and enduring commitment. Catholic scholar Paul M. Conner notes there have been close cross-sex friendships in "every period of Christian history."[2] These relationships are powerful witnesses of a sexual beauty between men and women who are passionately committed to love each other as Christ has loved them. They testify to the important difference between sex and sexuality. I can only speak from my limited experience, but it seems common for many Christians to narrow the meaning of sexuality to sex or everything revolving around genital sexuality.

Chaste cross-sex friendships cannot flourish in communities that limit sexuality to sex or to lust management. The stories of intimate but nonromantic cross-sex friendships help us to see our sexual theology in the Christian community has been too constricting and legalistic. As men and women made in the image of the triune God, there is a beauty in *friendship* as well as marriage. There is a wider and deeper social dimension to sexuality in God's world beyond the limited and narrow sexuality portrayed in the romantic myth and in popular culture. Romantic love does not have a monopoly on all deep love stories between men and women. What would male-female relationships look like in marriages and friendship if every man and woman could know the spiritual richness and beauty of oneness between genders? What would our churches look like if men and women sought deep communion with God and with each other?

CHAPTER 1

SACRED SEXUALITY AND FRIENDSHIP

In this sense, friendship between the sexes
may take us not out of ourselves
but beyond ourselves - may make us more whole,
more balanced and sane, than we could otherwise be.
Indeed, I myself think that this is one of the purposes of friendship....
We are being prepared ultimately
for that vast friendship which is in heaven,
in which we truly are taken beyond ourselves
and which all share in the love of God.

Gilbert Meilaender[1]

I have close friendships with three women: a single woman, a married woman, and my wife of twenty-eight years. I had no idea that my relationships with these two other women would plunge me into the mystery and depths of love, sexuality, and divine friendship.

These friendships became the subject of a conversation I had with my former pastor. Even though Sheila (my wife) fully supported these friendships, he said to me, "Dan, you're playing with fire! Men and women are hard-wired for sexual union when they enjoy intimacy with each other."

I just listened as he continued.

"The exceptions are familial intimacy, such as a close bond between mother and son, or brother and sister. Look at Genesis one and two; it's all there. Dan, look at Scripture," he pleaded. "Men and women are designed to experience intimacy and are wired to be one flesh."

He continued arguing his case using negative example after negative example. Now in some sense, who in their right mind would argue with him? According to my former pastor I was flying in the face of all Christian tradition and wisdom. It is my guess that for some Christians this same script is played in many private conversations over the phone, at Starbucks, in the pastor's study, or over the breakfast table. I was hoping (as was my wife) for a response different from the cut-and-dried, stereotypical reaction our rector gave.

At the time, my pastor did not even know the specifics of my intimate, cross-sex friendships. For several years my single friend and I have conversed with each other and with God about our anxieties and longings. We've prayed together for healing, job crises, graduate academic papers and stress, relational disconnects, her dating relationships, a place to live, car repairs, my marriage, ministry, our own relationship, sexual abuse, the death of her grandmother, the death of my mother, and everything in between. We've spent much time alone together and with my wife. We car-pooled together for eighteen months while we worked for the same company. During some stretches we've prayed daily with and for each other.

Yet, sex has not been an issue between us. Love, yes. Intimacy, yes. Sex, no.

If you are looking for a book which surveys the shifting relational practices and attitudes between genders in the contemporary Western world, issuing an appeal to return to a "Focus on the Family" 1950's value system with safe, predictable, distant, cut-and-dried boundaries to protect marriages and "family values," then this book might prove terrifying. However, if you are beginning to see there is more to male-female relationships than either marriage or extramarital sexual relationships this book is for you. Perhaps you think there must be something more for Christian men and women than the traditional way of assuming sex is an inevitable outcome when men and women get close. This book will help you on that journey. Some, no doubt, are going to fear the impact of such an idea; others will find it liberating.

Is Harry Right?

"What I'm saying," Harry looks at Sally in the popular 1989 romantic comedy, *When Harry Met Sally*, "and this is not a come-on in any way, shape or form, is that men and women can't be friends because the sex part always gets in the way."

Is Harry right? Many Christians use Harry's line as an infallible, uncontestable statement of the obvious to end further dialogue on the possibilities of deep friendship between men and women. Countless books have been written on the themes of protecting and enhancing the purity of genital sexuality, but little has been written by Protestants in the area of sexuality and close male-female friendships. For the most part, conservative Christian books on sexuality focus almost exclusively on marital sexuality and spirituality. Some authors are beginning to at least mention the value of transmarital cross-sex friendships, but Western culture in general portrays male-female relationships as a stepping stone to romantic relationships or marriage. In such a culture, married men and women may perceive close friendships with members of the opposite sex as threatening. Eight years into close friendships with women, I am convinced there is an often unmentioned sweet and passionate reality that is transformative, intimate, and authentic—a way of embodied intimacy between a man and woman who are not married to each other.

Authors John Scudder and Anne Bishop fit that description. They have enjoyed a deep friendship for decades. They describe such closeness between men and women:

> Relationships between men and women that do not involve romance and sex are usually referred to as 'just' friend relationships. Unlike 'just' friend relationships, rich personal relationships between the sexes have been overlooked. Most people are aware that 'just' friend relationships can become affairs, but few people seem aware that 'just' friend relationships can blossom into relationships of dialogical love. Those of us who have experienced the abundant being that can come from a deep personal relationship with a

person of the opposite sex would never speak of our relationship as 'just' Calling these relationships 'just' friends is not only misleading; it trivializes the relationship in a way that seems sacrilege.[2]

Victor Luftig in his book *Seeing Together: Friendship Between the Sexes in English Writing* highlights this awkwardness which he says shapes conversations about nonromantic male-female friendships toward *"what it is not."*[3] Indeed, to suggest any positive affirmation of a close male-female friendship immediately invites suspicion. Luftig suggests that "what is being talked about is in fact not friendship but sex, whether unacknowledged, unrealized, or unrevealed. To begin defining friendship according to the absence of sex may be to say much about one's expectations concerning gender relations, but it is also to offer little hope for being able to say what friendship actually is."[4]

Luftig further suggests that authentic stories of intimate friendships between men and women who do not include sex in their journeys threaten traditional ideas about how men and women relate when they get close. According to the entrenched stereotypes, stories of close friendships with the other gender must always end in romance, as in the conclusion of *When Harry Met Sally*. Since this is a *romantic* comedy, the movie has to end with Harry and Sally falling in love with each other. According to John Scudder, many in our sexualized culture believe that "it would make no sense to say that couples became friends in order to not have sex."[5] So Luftig asks, "How can a story remain genuinely *about* friendship, rather than position friendship as a merely temporary stage on the way to something the story is more essentially about?"[6] He observes, "Friendship between men and women, no matter how intensely valued by how many people, is scarcely nameable as a thing unto itself."[7]

Is Harry right? What if Harry is wrong? What if sexuality is so much more than Harry's vision of male-female intimacy? Is it possible that Christian friendship between a man and woman is an authentic, embodied witness pointing to a greater reality than the image offered by romantic comedies? Perhaps a subversive aspect of Christian discipleship should be the intentional formation and nurture of embodied spiritual friendships in order to present a witness which counters traditional assumptions about male-female relationships. Embodied spiritual friendship includes cultivating the well-being of the other, delighting in their gendered presence, and sharing hugs, food, drink, work, ministry, and play.

Jesus intentionally met with women. He traveled with them, and shared intimate, private conversations with them. In the presence of others, he pursued new social possibilities thought inappropriate by religious leaders. Although conservative Christians may be reluctant or fearful and choose to resist such, broad, rich, embodied relational possibilities, Lilian Calles Barger suggests:

> Our society is centered on either the containment of sex or reducing all needs to the erotic ... people are looking not for a no-holds-barred sexuality but for a sexuality to be defined more broadly than the erotic. The flagrant sexuality of MTV and sitcoms gives us a reduction of the expansive life-affirming motivation that our sexuality is. But people are longing for a broadening of what it means to be a sexual person.[8]

What does the Christian story have to say about what it means to be a male sexual being or a female sexual being? What does it mean for a Christian man who desires a strong and close relationship with his wife, but who also desires to relate to other women out of a sexuality which goes beyond the conventional paths of romance, inappropriate sex, or fearful avoidance?

Cross-Sex Communion

Conservative Christianity pours much energy into stressing the sacredness of the mysterious union between husband and wife. "Sexuality," writes Lewis Smedes, "is the human drive toward intimate communion."[9] Describing marital sex, Rob Bell states, "What goes on between them is a profound mystery. The mystery of the mingling of souls."[10] Many contemporary Christians would agree with Mike Mason, that "socially, legally, physically, emotionally, there is just no other means of getting closer to another human being, and never has been, than in marriage."[11] He is right. They all are.

Any suggestion of an embodied communion between unmarried men and women is often seen as a threat to the mysterious, ongoing, passionate bond between husband and wife. Forming and nurturing a close, embodied friendship openly between sexes may raise suspicion, awkwardness, and fears and therefore elicit external social pressure from the community beyond the marriage. "Audience" suspicions may generate widespread, though unwarranted and sinful gossip, thereby pressuring some well-meaning friends to avoid innocent outings or engage in only chaperoned interaction without close, public affection. Is the male-female bond in marriage the *only* embodied relationship in male-female sexuality to experience *communion* on this side of heaven? Is it possible there are assumptions about sexuality, love, marriage, and authentic Christian community in paired female-male friendships we need to rethink?

While there is no question the Bible portrays marriage as a passionate and exclusive genital communion, the Bible is also persuasively clear that the marital communion is taken up in a greater and broader communion: the communion of God and the saints. The entire collective Christian community affirms that marital sexuality points to a reality beyond itself. Rob Bell has it right when he says, "Central to the Bible is the affirmation that there is one God. Not many, one. And sex between the man and woman has something to do with God. Who God is. What God is like. Adam and Eve are one as God is one. Same word."[12] When Jesus came into this world, he radically challenged every Jew who believed with their whole heart and culture that God was one. Many Jews believed Jesus was undermining their core belief: one God. After Jesus' resurrection, the apostles declared: "Yet for us there is one God, the Father, from whom are all things and for whom we exist, and one Lord, Jesus Christ, through whom are all things and through whom we exist" (1 Cor. 8:6). This one God leads us all (including both married couples and singles) into the mystery of communion with the triune Community and with *others*—both men and women. Miroslav Volf describes it: "Salvation is communion with God and human beings."[13] Jesus prayed for this deep relational communion for us, far greater and broader than married communion alone:

> I ask not only on behalf of these, but also on behalf of those who will believe in me through their word, that they may all be one. As you, Father, are in me and I am in you, may they also be in us, so that the world may believe that you have sent me. The glory that you have given me I have given them, so that they may be one, as we are one, I in them and you in me, that they may become completely one, so that the world may know that you have sent me and have loved them even as you have loved me. (John 17:20-23)

This "oneness," too, is a social "mystery" in the New Testament. Marriage is not the only social relationship where the mystery of embodied spiritual communion is present. Although Paul doesn't explicitly use the word "mystery" in Galatians 3:28 as he does for marriage in Ephesians 5:32, theologians for two millennia have been plumbing the social, relational, spiritual and physical ramifications of male and female who are now "one" in Christ. Something utterly profound has happened in Christ regarding male and female relationships (not just between husband and wife) in this present age and the one to come: "There is no longer Jew or Greek, there is no longer slave or free, there is no longer male and female; for all of you are one in Christ Jesus" (Galatians 3:28).

Protestant vs. Catholic Views of Friendship

It may surprise some that in Catholic spirituality friendship may reach a mutual communion—a mystic union of "two-in-one" intimacy. Rarely has such a mystical union of friendship been explored in Protestant ecclesiology and spirituality. For centuries evangelicals and fudamentalists have not had a theology or a spirituality for such friendship intimacy, and therefore lacked interest in birthing and nurturing friendship as embodied communion—same-gender or cross-gender. Evangelical spirituality has focused on the word of God preached or privately read and our response to it. Long before public gay affection, many Protestant men felt uneasy about the virtue of desire and intimacy in personal friendships. Romantic or married love in contemporary western Protestant culture is viewed as the primary and sometimes exclusive path to affectionate, deep interpersonal love between two people. I single out Protestants because there have been significant Catholic and Eastern Orthodox voices which have recognized and named friendship-love as another kind of embodied, mystical communion. Catholic scholar Louis Colin writes of friendship: "May we not define it as the mystical marriage of two souls in search of God? Has it not in fact something of that sacrament in it: total and mutual giving, intimacy, faithfulness, indissolubility, fecundity? ... It is a union of two souls."[14]

Carmen Caltagirone, a contemporary Catholic author and spiritual director, writing on intimacy in friendship says, "With our soul mates we share the experience of knowing and being known. Heart speaks to heart and two are bonded together and become one."[15] By "soul mates" she means an intentional, close bond between two friends in a nonromantic friendship. John Bonnici, another Catholic writer, describes friendship as "a manifestation of interpersonal communion."[16] Eastern Orthodox theologian Paul D. O'Callaghan writes of friendship: "The experience of human friendship is that in which full persons achieve genuine communion in the one human nature."[17]

While not a widespread phenomenon, Catholic scholar Paul Conner points out that there have been intimate, "fulfilling and complementing friendships between saintly men and women in every period of Christian history."[18] In a chapter entitled "Two-in-One," Conner surveyed several male-female friendships in church history and summarized them:

> While always ordered to God, the friendship between these men and women was fully and deeply human, bringing them to experience a spiritual unity of two-in-one-love. They were constantly present to one another in mind and heart. Personally

or by letter they shared in full trust the intimate details of their human and spiritual lives. They admired each other's qualities and virtues and openly expressed a unique, intense affection for one another. Each was ever anxious for another's human and supernatural welfare. Both suffered from separation and rejoiced singularly when they were together or could at least receive letters from each other.[19]

Evangelicals have been uneasy recognizing such interpersonal communion in friendship. Theologians, particularly Protestant theologians, have virtually ignored any significant theological relationship between divine love and friendship love. C.S. Lewis, a respected evangelical scholar quoted frequently in discussions on friendships, used a gendered, masculine definition of friendship when he wrote about the distinction between friendship love as being "side-by-side" and romantic love as "face-to-face."

However, mainstream evangelical author Ruth Barton wonders about how "safe" sex-segregated boundaries among male-female relationships may prevent emotional, physical, and spiritual intimacy in faith communities:

> If men and women are not free to share thoughts and ideas over lunch, if we cannot talk with enough privacy and safety to work through issues, if we cannot spend enough time together that we feel like we know each other, if we cannot have fun together, if we cannot open our hearts and love each other as friends do, we will keep a safe distance that permits us to communicate only over a chasm of apathy, misunderstanding and inadequate information.[20]

Alongside the resistance to communion in friendships has been a widespread emphasis on the private individual. The beginning of the evangelical conversion story centers on the experience of a private and isolated decision to follow Christ. This focus on a privatized spirituality continues as the evangelical sub-culture stresses how our evangelical identity is found in "quiet times," or our commitment to private prayer and Bible reading. The *isolated* experience tends to be the high point for evangelical spirituality. In fact, evangelical theologians and pastors have encouraged, exhorted, and entreated Christians to depend on God *alone* as their helper, deliverer, burden bearer, refuge, strength, encourager, friend, and counselor. Scores of books have been written on the virtue and benefit of private, isolated, withdrawn, personal prayer. With this inordinate emphasis on the individual, it is rare to find an evangelical who values formation from paired friendship love and community.

What may be authentic, holy, healthy stirrings, and longings of a man toward a woman (or a woman toward a man) in embodied friendship love may find opposition from evangelical communities, even if one's spouse welcomes the friendship. Delighting in and desiring the other's gendered presence is more than just friendliness; rather it can be a healthy desire in male-female sexuality. As notes Lewis Smedes, "Sexuality has to do with *much more than* genital sex" (italics added).[21] The desire for meaningful delight in another's *gendered* embodied presence may not be a sign of weakness or flirtation with promiscuity, but rather an indication that one is grounded in an authentic, "thick" understanding of Christian male-female relations.

Transmarital Social Mystery

Male-female relations include a transmarital social mystery. "Mysteries," according to Gordon Hilsman, are "aspects of reality that must be entered into in order to be realized and endlessly unfold without ever being completely mastered."[22] Speaking of cross-sex friendships Smedes writes:

> When a man and woman enter each other's lives, their separate mysteries almost immediately begin to unfold to each other. And as they begin to unveil their mysteries, they are taken into an emotional flow that will carry them to places neither of them has been before. The woman has hidden reservoirs of feeling and need she has not yet explored. The man has emotional resources he has never come to feel. Unsuspected yearnings, unexplored needs, and untapped feelings begin to unfold. Each has a mystery moving

within waiting to be evoked, and once evoked, it opens the door to still more untapped mysteries.[23]

In Genesis 2, Adam is awakened, discovers Eve, and he immediately proclaims, "This at last is bone of my bones and flesh of my flesh" (Genesis 2:23). Click that pause button. Hold it. Don't move to the next verse yet. Although it is patently clear that this primal story refers to genital intimacy, it would be premature to define all male-female relations as a stepping stone to genital intimacy based solely on this exclamation from Adam. Most evangelicals—most conservatives—have a tendency to read Adam's statement as an ancient form of verbal foreplay because of the following verse, "Therefore a man leaves his father and his mother and clings to his wife, and they become one flesh" (Genesis 2:24).

The immediate context for Adam (a very long day of naming animals) meant he was seeing Eve after having seen all the other animals that were paraded before him in the Garden. His response was a deep expression of inexplicable connectedness. This was not a proclamation *after* sex; indeed, there is no indication Adam and Eve immediately had sex after he said this. It was a reaction of inexplicable interconnectedness the first time he laid eyes on Eve. The temptation, of course, is to sexualize all male-female relationships, including friendships.

But if we hit the pause button long enough between Genesis 2:23 and Genesis 2:24, we may come to the unfathomable, impenetrable, transcendental mystery of Aristotle's "another self" in Christian male-female relations. Again, there is no question that genital intimacy between male and female emerges in the Garden of Eden story, but theologian David Carr in his book *The Erotic Word: Sexuality and Spirituality and the Bible* observes:

> This is not to suggest that we do or should sexualize all of our relationships, nor that all life should be seen through the lens of genital sexuality. Instead, this text's words about human earthiness, the divine breath in us, and human intimacy can encourage us to broaden our appreciation of the role of passion in human life

as a whole. This text can help us recognize the myriad ways in which our relationships and longings in life are, to various extents, already erotic.[24]

Theologian Elaine Storkey wisely assesses the cultural atmosphere which results when we have a one-size-fits-all model for male-female relations:

Our sex-crazed culture suggests that any form of cross-sex intimacy must inevitably lead to the bedroom. And so a deep fear of sexuality is often projected which presents it as so engulfing that it will contaminate any relationships unless regulated firmly by marriage. Consequently, any unmarried woman who maintains close contact with a married man friend is seen as suspect, and possibly even promiscuous. These are anxieties expressed towards his wife, and about the trustworthiness of the husband. The unmarried friend can easily be seen as the 'other woman', even when friendship is innocent of any kind of unfaithfulness. Equally doubtful are friendships between people married to different partners. The fear is always that the relationship could intensify and compete with the marriages. Therefore people are often advised that the safest thing is to maintain only superficial relationships with others outside of marriage, and look to one's partner for all the friendship needed.[25]

There are a growing number of Christians who agree with Storkey about the need to move on from a fear-based sexuality where men and women are uncomfortable or uneasy about practicing a face-to-face, social intimacy—that is, not just polite friendliness or neighborliness, but an intentionally seeking out the other for prayer, support, food, play, and socializing. "Many Christians," comments Ruth Haley Barton on this subject, "respond to their sexuality with a mixture of denial, judgment, fear and guilt."[26] Catholic theologian Ronald Rolheiser writes, "Deep, intimate, chaste heterosexual friendship is no small achievement," but he says friendships that are deep are, "worth the risk and effort."[27]

CHAPTER 2

ROMANTIC MYTH AND FRIENDSHIP

"In so many ways our culture trains us to be unfit for friendship."

Paul Wadell[1]

If you were living in the Chicago area during the spring of 1988, you may recall the story of Wheaton College students Scott Swanson and Carolyn MacLean. On April 2, 1988, these two unmarried, mainstream evangelical college students from upper middle class families suddenly vanished in Chicago. Their BMW was found in an alley. Their parents were deeply concerned that something tragic had happened to them during one of their romantic evenings in Chicago. Their sudden disappearance launched a search involving three states. There was nowhere to turn in Chicago without seeing or hearing media coverage in the first week of April. Six weeks into their disappearance, a *New York Times* article stated, "Six weeks ago today 23-year-old Scott Swanson and 22-year-old Carolyn MacLean vanished in a case that has tortured their families and baffled the police here." In June 1988, they were discovered living in San Diego. Carolyn, couching their motives with the language of romantic myth infused with Christian spirituality, said, "We're so in love and we wanted to get away from the adornment and the material world and develop our relationship together apart from that." Scott said, "We feel like we're on a different level than a lot of people. Carolyn's my life, and me to her, her to me. I would die for her and she would die for me."

Totally absorbed in their own romantic world, they craved making a new world completely revolving around their selves to the extent they left everyone including their families in deep anguish searching for them for weeks. Laura Smit in her book, *Loves Me, Loves Me Not*, comments: "Our culture generally elevates the romantic experience of falling in love above religious commitment, teaching us that this emotional experience is both beyond our control and beyond all reproach."[2] Idealizing romantic passion as the unique, one-and-only, exclusive form of love between a man and woman has created a pervasive romantic myth in our contemporary world when it comes to male-female paired relationships. Kathy Werking, a pioneering scholar in cross-sex friendship notes: "Romantic relationships are celebrated as an ideal woman-man relationship in our society. The myths of our culture secure a special status for romantic heterosexual relationships since these myths idealize romantic love and promote the notion that the emotional well-being of men and women is dependent upon their involvement in a 'successful' romantic relationship."[3]

Many people—Christian and non-Christian—wrestle with their self-esteem and self-worth if they are not participating in a romantic relationship. They find it utterly depressing to be excluded from such a relationship. Not surprisingly for Christians, they question God's personal and intimate goodness towards them, their stories, their embodied selves, their sexual selves, their desires, their hopes, and their dreams. But, it doesn't stop there. The romantic myth ironically undermines self-esteem and worth among those *within* romantic relationships, too. Conservative Christians reinforce this idealization when they portray romantic love as the *total* giving of self in this one male-female relationship. In the romantic myth, "Love and sexuality are fused together in the ideology of romance."[4]

This is the fruit of romantic idealism, not romantic realism. The notion that one idealized relationship is the be-all, end-all for passion, intimacy, emotional commitment, friendship, happiness, fidelity, and depth, has a cluster of powerful myths supporting it within the evangelical community.

Myths of Romantic Idealism

Myth 1: "One flesh" satisfies our deepest yearnings for oneness.
In a culture where romantic love is a multi-billion dollar business with no end in sight, it is a challenging but *necessary* calling for Christians to affirm that the "one flesh" of marriage holds deep meaning. But while affirming the passion, love, and fidelity of marriage, we must reject the notion that "one flesh" justifies a self-absorbed, romantic idealism. Romantic passion is not at stake here. Neither is exclusive sexual union. Such passion from time to time is right and good in marriage. Romantic idealism is something different. Mark Vernon picks up on this romantic idealism when he writes: "In today's world, there is a myth of romantic love based upon two lovers becoming one flesh, a totalisation of life in the other, supremely enacted in sexual ecstasy which is symbolic of that union."[5] This "totalisation of life" in the evangelical sub-culture is zealously reinforced by well-meaning Christians when the notion of "leaving and cleaving" is interpreted through the lens of the modern romantic myth, making all other "unions," including friendship, peripheral.

The Christianized version of the romantic myth exaggerates, idealizes, and isolates the path of dating or courtship to marriage as the only prize in paired male-female relationships under the justification of "one flesh." Embodied knowledge, relational depth, emotional closeness, physical tenderness, sensual warmth and play, vulnerability, trust, fidelity, commitment, union, spontaneity, understanding, giving the utmost— these dynamic *nongenital* relational qualities are romanticized and sexualized under the evangelical rhetoric of one flesh. Some Christians who see these dynamics in male-female pairs presume this "couple" must be on the path toward romantic and genital intimacy.

Oneness and sexuality have become synonyms.

A powerful belief in some Christian circles is that God has a particular soulmate for us. Our soulmate is the one man or woman God has designed for us, for our happiness, for our well-being here on earth. When we meet him or her for the first time, we will experience an instant connection. We marry that special someone and live happily ever after in true love with our soulmate. For these Christians the romantic myth is infused with finding and keeping our soulmate for life—a search that may equal religious devotion. Frank Tallis, author of the book, *Love Sick: Love as a Mental Illness*, suggests, "Romanticism is the closest thing we have to a religious faith in a predominantly secular society. This is probably because love is frequently associated with intense experiences of rapture and ecstasy."[6]

It is expected in Christian communities as well as in movies and popular culture that love-saturated men and women will pair off exclusively from the rest of their world, to pursue almost infinite emotional and mental intensity. They might not suddenly vanish like Scott and Carolyn did, but couples buy this myth in the Western culture because "everyone raves about it and they want to be sure they are not missing something important."[7] At its greatest peak, romantic love incessantly craves total emotional, intellectual, physical, and sexual union. The ideal romantic love, Helen Fisher reminds us, is "the craving for sexual gratification; and *attachment*—the feelings of calm, security, and union with a long-term partner."[8] In the myth, male-female relationships beyond the marriage are seen as a threat to this idealized pairing. For some well-intentioned Christian communities, the fusion of one flesh with romantic myth has driven some to draw exclusive boundaries about oneness and marriage.

Edwin Young in his book, *Romancing the Home: How to Have a Marriage that Sizzles*, likens one flesh to a "private little castle"[9] in a chapter on "Why Marriages Fizzle." He believes that marriages are threatened "when a door or window to the private little castle of marriage is left open, and family, friends, and neighbors are allowed to enter in."[10]

In the context, it appears Young is referring to the relational intimacy within this "private little castle" which ought to be off limits to anyone except professional help. He asserts, "Your marriage is a private castle that is sacred, sheltered, and secluded."[11] Deep, sacred friendships (same-sex or cross-sex) of oneness entering into the "one flesh" of marriage are strongly discouraged by Young. Instead of seriously critiquing and engaging the romantic idealism, he seems to anoint the romantic myth using Christian language of one flesh to support it.

For centuries Christians have *yearned* for oneness, but they craved this communion through friendship, community, and sometimes, but not always, marriage. Before Sigmund Freud's impact on friendship, the language of desire was central in nonromantic relationships as well as in marriage. Although some contemporary Christians now distance themselves from such stark passion in friends, passionately desiring your friend's presence was once a sign of flourishing friendship. Consider the depth of passion expressed between Christian friends prior to romantic idealism:

The Church father, St. Basil the Great to a close friend: "It is impossible for me to forget you even for the briefest moment— I would sooner forget myself."[12]

Paulinus to Severus: "We have one heart and soul together in the Lord." In another place, he states, "For we always loved each other so scrupulously that no affection could be added to our mutual love except the charity of Christ."[13]

Augustine reflecting on a friend: "I felt that his soul and mine had formed one soul in two bodies."[14]

Elmer (1128-37), a monk, to a friend: "I cannot tell you, my most beloved, with what sweetness, with what efficacy of spiritual desire, my mind embraces your soul in the intimacy of holy love, when it remembers gently your goodness."[15]

Peter, a monk, to a friend, Bernard: "And so it is always something sweet for us to speak with you, and to keep a honeyed sweetness between us in our love through joyful talks."[16]

Franciscan Bernardino of Siena (1380-1444) eulogizing his friend, Vincent: "He was always so closely united to me and loved me with all his soul. In religion he was an older brother to me; in love he was another self."[17]

William Wirt, husband, lawyer, and Christian, to longtime friend Dabney Carr: "I long for your hand—I hunger for your face and voice."[18]

Emily Shore, writing in her diary in 1862 about her friend: "She was sitting up in bed, looking so sweet and lovely that I could not take my eyes off her."[19]

This was the language of oneness in Christian friendship for *centuries*. Passages like Acts 4:32 shaped how Christian leaders viewed friendship: "Now the whole group of those who believed were of one heart and one soul, and no one claimed private ownership of any possessions, but everything was held in common." Ambrose, Bishop of Milan in the fourth century, extols union in friendship: "What is a friend, but a partner in love? You unite your innermost being to his, you join so thoroughly with him that your aim is to be no longer two, but one."[20]

Could it be that when strict exclusionary boundaries of the romantic myth are at the heart of Christian marriage, it becomes vulnerable to the failure of the perfect soulmate dream? Rarely does the intensity of the myth last—for many reasons. People change. Relationships do not remain the same. The joy of romantic idealism wears off. Passion wears off. There may be gnawing doubts that perhaps we married the wrong person and are now stuck. It may happen that a powerful new attraction begins to feed doubts about the marriage and the friendship between husband and wife. The myth does not tolerate a "loveless" (i.e., the absence of romantic passion) marriage. In 2009, some in the national media urged South Carolina Governor Mark Sanford to divorce his wife because he was passionately in love with Maria Belen Chapur. Bonnie Fuller counsels Sanford, "If you are truly and passionately in love with the Argentinean Maria, why ruin several lives by denying it. You're not doing your wife, Jenny, any favors by resigning yourself to a marriage that's no longer working."[21] Firmly embedded in the romantic myth is the belief that we can only be happy if we are "in love" with our ideal soulmate. David Matzko McCarthy correctly points out the inevitability that occurs in this narrative: "falling in love makes a relationship true."[22]

This idealism sounds wonderful at the beginning, as McCarthy observes, but "marriage would have to be so heroic as to carry the weight of a total self, or the self would have to be shallow and one dimensional, so that it could be completely unveiled in a single relationship."[23] This myth is unhealthy, if not unsustainable over the course of time. "Intense romantic passion consumes enormous energy and time."[24] When it is not present, a spouse may yearn for excitement, adventure, and the "true" soulmate. Those caught up in the myth are susceptible to stress and disillusionment both before marriage (singles who feel they are desperately missing this idealized experience) and within marriage (spouses who are tempted to pursue greener pastures outside of marriage).

Myth 2: One flesh satisfies our deepest yearnings for sexuality

In the Western world, sex has not been the same since Freud. Whatever opinions we have about Freud, there is no disputing that he put sexual energy squarely in the center of relationality and behavior. Freud attributed many physical behaviors to underlying sexual drives. He genitalized affection, physical tenderness, gestures, and desires even between biological brothers and sisters. Freud genitalized all sensuality—not just foreplay. He genitalized emotional closeness and depth.

Sexual formation in our post-Freudian culture is primarily about genital sex. Jean Kilbourne states that, "advertising and the popular culture define human connection almost entirely in terms of sex, thus overemphasizing the relative importance of sex in our lives (and marriages) and underemphasizing the other important things (friendship, loyalty, fun, love of children, community)."[25]

In many Christian communities a positive sexuality has been sequestered into either marriage or the idealized romantic relationship as a stepping stone to marriage. The result? By and large, the church seems to send the same message as the sex-saturated media: romantic sexuality in all its fullness is sufficient for communion. We live in an age in which the romantic path towards sex is set apart both in the culture and in many Christian communities as the be-all and end-all of our earthly experience. As James Loder notes, "The great sex charade is the popular celebration in the media and in our society and culture at large of sexuality as the major indicator of intimacy between persons."[26] While Christian tradition has certainly had a checkered past with its fear of sex, perhaps the pendulum has swung far into the romantic myth narrative when it comes to sexuality and communion.

Consider the conversation currently taking place between the haves and the have-nots when it comes to sex: those who are married and those who are not. In their book, *Singled Out*, Christine Colón and Bonnie Field identify several key messages in popular Christian teaching: "Individuals are incomplete without marriage/sex; sex is a form of prayer; and sex is the primary means through which we experience the divine." They add, "Such messages that glorify sex certainly suggest that singles cannot know God as well as those who are married because we are not experiencing the shekinah glory in the marital bed and we are not sharing the image of God through procreation."[27] They believe that "Christians complain about the world's obsession with sex, but it seems like some churches have given in to the obsession."[28]

In the romantic myth on this side of Freud, then, many Christians believe a man or a woman should only *desire* to be *one* with their romantic partner or spouse. Here we again encounter the romantic assumption that oneness and sex are synonyms—exclusively. Many Christian communities don't have a robust, positive view of sexuality and communion beyond the romantic couple. What does it mean to be in communion with another, as men and women? In the romantic myth there is only one answer for all men and women. Romantic love and sexual union trumps all else when it comes to communion.

Some naïve Christians may be tempted to see good sex as full, complete intimacy given the church's emphasis, while singles feel left out of God's unique blessings for them as sexual beings. Yet, as many pastoral caregivers can attest, there are couples who get divorced even though they believe they have a good sex life. There are couples who have sex even though they are experiencing major relational difficulties with each other. The sex in some Christian marriages may fall far short of accomplishing the idealized communion popular evangelical teaching says it will.

Could it be that in so emphasizing a positive view of sexuality in the narrow context of romantic pairing, Christian communities have missed profound, embodied spiritual intimacy in *other* sacred unions— friendships? It is at this point that the language of communion, union, oneness, passion, and delight, drastically drops off the relational radar screen in our post-Freudian world. Loder suggests that, "The sex charade appears and thrives in church life as in the world because we do not know how nor do we have the theological nerve to investigate the depth of spiritual intimacy that we want in all of our leaders and fellow members in the koinonia."[29]

Faith communities influenced by Freud's ideas are likely to be deeply suspicious of the formation of any male-female friendship pairing that does not have freedom for an appropriate romantic trajectory. The French philosopher Paul Ricoeur described Freud as a "master of suspicion." By Freudian default, desiring a close cross-sex friend is to be interpreted as having primal genital interest in that "friend" whether either person is cognizant of it or not. For Christians impacted by Freud, husbands and wives have no other outlet for richness in sexuality and relationality besides each other. How could there be? Any attraction towards another's beauty or physical affection or shared physical tenderness is latent with genital drives and must be wisely avoided. In Freud's world, there can be no richness, beauty, order, depth, or communion between men and women in transmarital friendships, because repressed sexual desire is present in all male-female closeness. All intimacy has been primarily eroticized, and therefore only the romantic relationship of "one flesh" is able to enter the wild depths of passionate communion.

Joseph Epstein, in his book *Friendship: An Expose*, is among many who believe that if Freud's theories are taken seriously, they "would just about eliminate friendship altogether. Eroticizing everything, as is their wont, Freudians find that much close male friendship is at its core homoerotic, while the notion of male-female friends outside sexual interest is generally inconceivable to Freudians, who not so secretly believe that all men wish to do with women is jump their bones."[30] Another contemporary author, Lisa Gee, a contemporary author who is critical of the Freudian legacy, comments on the genitalization in Freud's theories: "When Freud spoke of and wrote about sex, he wasn't only referring to acts tending towards copulation, or those which are what most of think of as consciously sexual … anything physically (or mentally) pleasurable counts as sexual."[31]

Yet, the story of Christ must not allow Freud to have the final word on sexuality and friendship. Later, we shall see in greater detail how Jesus himself received physical pleasure from women in the context of friendships. There are more and more compelling stories in contemporary society of physically affectionate, flourishing cross-sex friendships with no romantic motivations. Lisa Gee explains:

> Although for lots of heterosexual male-female pairs, physical expressions of affection may function primarily as a preliminary to sex … many other people—brothers and sisters, parents and children, friends—are physically affectionate without a hint of sexual arousal. They hug each other. They kiss. We may put a comforting hand on a distressed friend's back, or offer a real shoulder to cry on. As children we might have been stroked or cuddled to sleep, and we might still enjoy the same thing as adults.[32]

Myth 3: One flesh satisfies our yearnings for deep friendship
Friendship, like sex, has not been the same since Freud. In the post-Freud world, the romantic myth *requires* your spouse to be your best friend and requires that all other friendships be incidental. How could it be otherwise? Both secular and Christian thinkers see Freudian flaws embedded in the romantic myth. We interpret physical and emotional closeness in friendship through a Freudian lens, and therefore, whether we acknowledge it or not, make marriage the romantic male-female pairing *the* model for love. When emotional, spiritual, and physical depth of love is latent with erotic impulses and primal sexual drives, then the only deep relationship of love available to men and women with the conservative Christian view of sexuality is male-female romantic pairing.

When Christian communities make Freud's view of sexuality (even modified) and the romantic myth "compatible" with their biblical principles, the idealization of marriage becomes coherent with the rejection of intimate male-female friendship beyond marriage or outside of marriage: all the gestures, pleasures, emotions, and desires of *nonromantic* love are genitalized on this side of Freud. Although there is no question Freud's views have been modified through the years, both secular and Christian thinkers who embrace psychodynamic theory see sexuality as a powerful drive in male-female relationships. As Lisa McMinn comments: "Although Freud has been misunderstood and criticized for saying so, he saw sexual energy as the life force that motivates all human behavior."[33]

When conservative Christians adapt a modified Freudian view of sexuality and conflate the romantic myth with the meaning of one flesh, one wonders how Christian husbands and wives are able to pursue deep intimacy and become companions on the marital journey. Perhaps the greatest enemy of marriage when the notion of one flesh has been made synonymous with the romantic myth is the one flesh vision of marriage itself. When the romantic myth makes sex and romantic passion the end of marriage, it creates impossible standards. As Tallis notes, in romantic idealism "we unwittingly expect love to deliver the kind of happiness that was associated with a direct experience of the numinous. In effect, we look to another human being to give life meaning and purpose."[34] He observes that a core assumption in romantic idealism is that life is not satisfactory without our ideal soulmate. The popular culture feeds this illusion by wedding passionate sex and romantic relationships. Sex in the popular culture is all about passion and technique. We are over-saturated with advice in magazines and on the internet presenting advice on how to rev up sexual ecstasy. Lauren Winner in her book, *Real Sex*, wonders if, "We've defined sex as something unsustainable—bodice ripping, stupefying and nightly."[35] One of the greatest vulnerabilities of the romantic myth is that it transforms ordinary people into extraordinary lovers *for a period of time*. Once the period of obsession wanes, one morning the spouses may wake up and come to the settled conclusion they are not "in love" anymore.

Rodney Clapp believes Christians have to pursue something greater than romantic idealism in marriage. In an article entitled, "Why Christians Have Lousy Sex Lives," he suggests, "The important question for Christians, then, after five, ten, fifty years of marriage, is not, 'Am I still in love with my spouse?' The better question is, "Are we stronger, deeper, continuing Christian friends?'"[36] While it's certainly debatable if that's the question that needs to be asked, it does suggest that the idealized romantic relationship itself is not able to satisfy the yearnings for deep friendship. This is where the romantic myth begins to surge forward and actually undermine classic spiritual friendship between the man and woman in marriage. We will see in later chapters there have been many deep, mutually satisfying friendships in Church history which lasted longer than many modern Christian marriages. Romantic idealism in our culture, even in the Christian sub-culture, has become the highest ideal, and yet almost fifty per cent of marriages end in divorce.

It's not surprising then, that for evangelicals caught up in the myth, nonromantic friendships is uninspiring and insignificant. This is the fruit of a post-Freud romantic culture in which gestures, winks, touches, kisses, caresses, massages, pleasure, delight, and beauty must be imbued with romantic energy, meaning, and importance. We have lost the spirituality of classical friendship as a calling in our life both before marriage, outside of marriage, and within marriage. Not all attraction is romanticized, not all beauty is romanticized, not all yearning for another is romanticized, not all physical pleasure is romanticized, and not all extraordinary closeness is romanticized. There is a "third way" of classical friendship—a way of spirituality and intimacy in which intimacy is not all about romance and genital expression.

Here, classical Christianity calls us out to something *much more* than the "much more" embedded in romantic idealism. God, who is love, calls us all—singles, husbands, wives, widows, widowers, divorced— into a spirituality of love and friendship in marriage, beyond marriage, and outside of marriage. While God honors and blesses the marriage bed, God does not confine delight, goodness, passion, attraction, beauty, sensuality, spontaneity, or creativity to the boundaries of married love. Jesus himself embodied these realities as a single man. The spirituality of love and friendship in classical Christianity does not give us a stark contrast between great mystery of marital love and uninspiring platonic friendship outside of marriage. Both in the Bible and in tradition, the spirituality of friendship is presented as hungering for the good, the beautiful, and the true. "The shared time and space of friendship," writes Philip Rolnick, "holds the expectation of the good. The relational space of friendship is sacred, holy and virtually ecclesiological." He writes that it is possible and desirable for friendship to "*go forward in pursuit of more* truth, beauty, and goodness so that ever greater gifts of self can be given and received" (italics added).[37] What would happen in our marriages if both husband and wife hungered for the good, beautiful, and true in their marriage and beyond?

In some Christian communities, desire for *much more* other than God is presented as lust for something else other than God himself. But Jesus himself tells us *blessed* are those who hunger and thirst for righteousness. Jesus urges us to seek first the kingdom. Jesus himself encourages us to ask, seek, and knock as we seek God and his goodness. The imagery in both the Old and New Testaments urges us to pursue the *much more* of God's good and beautiful generosity. "For the Lord your God is bringing you into a good land, a land with flowing streams, with springs and underground waters welling up in valleys and hills" (Deut. 8:7). In Psalm 36:7-8 we read, "How precious is your steadfast love, O God! All people may take refuge in the shadow of your wings. They feast on the abundance of your house, and you give them drink from the river of your delights." These images tap into a spirituality that hungers for much more in marriage *and* friendship.

The Bible, though, also presents us with a "much more" that we are not to hunger after, beginning in the Garden of Eden. Even though Adam and Eve had abundant fruit in the Garden to feast on, the serpent tempts them with something more. In reality, Adam and Eve had so much in the Garden, and in communion with God who is good, who is beautiful, who is true: they had *so much more to look forward to*. Yet, they chose the "more" beyond God's feast for them. In Christian spirituality, the sexual intimacy between a husband and wife is presented as a fountain and a spring (Prov. 5:16).

If it is possible in mutual delight, in mutual empowerment, in mutual desire to love each other distinctively in a Christian marriage, then a husband or wife might see a rich, meaningful, affectionate, and intimate love in cross-sex friendship as a gift from God and something morally excellent and beautiful for the sake of their spouse, community, and the kingdom. As Paul Wadell reminds us, the skill of mutual love is "the skill of being able to seek the good of another precisely because we have taken time to *discover* her as other and *discern* what respecting and responding to her 'otherness' requires."[38] This insight opens numerous possibilities for spiritual friendship to bring out each other's best in marriage, vocation, gifts, callings, and ministries.

These redemptive possibilities alongside the emergence of meaningful cross-sex friendships in contemporary society reveal there is a *much more* for singles in the communion of friendship. In the myth, singles not in romantic relationships are shut out from the richness and the depth of oneness, both in sexuality and spirituality. Although God created marriage and sexuality as a relationship where wild, deep intimacy abides, spiritual friendships between Christians are a different kind of communion that is also wild, deeply passionate, intimate, and fiercely loyal. Passion, goodness, affection, yearning, play, intensity, trust, and commitment are all accessible in spiritual friendships. Kenda Creasy Dean suggests, "The once sharp distinctions between *agape, philia*, and *eros*—Greek terms often used to distinguish selfless love, friendship love, and romantic love—have been muted by scholarly scrutiny. All love endures the fortunes of another; all love makes the lover vulnerable; all love suffers the weak-kneed hope of love returned."[39] There are friendships of sacred order in church history. They are the subject of our next chapter.

CHAPTER 3

SACRED ORDER AND FRIENDSHIP

*"Because of the complexity of the issue and individuals,
God does not give us a formula or rule book, although many try to implement
one, hoping for a guarantee. He asks us to develop a heart like his.
Following a formula is the Pharisee way—not the Jesus way."*

Sue Edwards[1]

In the middle of the night, Richard Loving and Mildred Jeter were summoned out of their bed and arrested by Sherriff R. Garnett Brooks. Their crime? They had exchanged wedding vows in Washington D.C. several weeks earlier in 1958. They loved each other and wanted to be married; he was a Caucasian while she was African American. Their home state of Virginia had a law against interracial marriage (as did fifteen other states at the time). The Virginia court system advocated "racial integrity" in personal relationships between men and women. It didn't matter that Loving and Jeter loved each other and wanted to be married.

For hundreds of years, interracial marriages held something in common with some popular perceptions of transmarital cross-sex friendships: they were socially inappropriate relationships deemed unbiblical and against the nature of the created order as the community understood it. Many Christian communities thought interracial marriages (and therefore dating) were reprehensible in the eyes of God, according to their reading of the Bible. Bob Jones University did not drop its ban on interracial dating until 2000.

Inappropriate. Taboo. Groundbreaking. Revolutionary. Against nature. Unconventional. Gossip. Risk. These words shaped discussion on interracial intimacy and therefore impacted social order in communities and personal relationships. But stories of interracial marriages among well-known Americans are shaping new relational and cultural maps. Both Barack Obama and Tiger Woods are offspring of interracial couples. This sense of racial inappropriateness in some personal relationships between two adults is not merely a Western Caucasian/ African American phenomenon. Interracial dating and marriage in many cultures challenge embedded cultural stereotypes in families, communities, and churches.

Social order of gender and race has been viewed by many Christian communities as an unarguable part of divine design rooted within creation or curse. In 1840, an Indiana state senator speaking about banning interracial marriage said:

> There is no subject which, in the present state of times, calls more loudly for legislative interposition than the one before them. It is an infraction of the laws of the Almighty, for one moment to allow the pernicious doctrine of such amalgamation to have an abiding place in our government, or upon our State books, being marked, as they are, by the eternal and unchangeable laws of God, the one white and the other black. Your committee believes that any man or set of men, who would encourage, counsel, or abet in such unholy marriages as said bill prohibits, deserve the just animadversion of every Christian philanthropist and patriot, and should be punished by several penalties imposed by legislative enactment.[2]

In 1865, in another case forbidding interracial marriage in Pennsylvania, the court ruled that "the right to be free from social contact is as clear as to be free from intermarriage. The former may be less repulsive as a condition, but no less entitled as a right."[3] Another bill in 1841 stated, "Gentlemen and ladies ... walking arm in arm with blacks in the public streets of the city! The insult to the people could not be resisted."[4] In 1942, an Ohio judge wrote: "The two races are placed as wide apart by hand of nature as white from black; and, to break down the barriers, fixed, as it were, by the Creator himself, in a political and social amalgamation, shocks us as something unnatural and wrong."[5]

Richard Loving and Mildred Jeter were not trying to launch a fresh civil rights movement when they married. In their biblical culture, what Richard and Mildred Loving wanted was understood to be against divine design and therefore utterly forbidden—a criminal act against the divine order for society and personal relationships. It is rare now for Christian institutions in America to forbid interracial dating or marriage. What seemed *unnatural* to the culture for generations is now accepted by many contemporary Christians as *good*.

Cross-sex friendships similarly challenge firmly held notions about appropriateness in personal relationships within contemporary evangelicalism. Many Christians assume *singular* purposes of order when interpreting the creation story. Transmarital cross-sex friendship stories are forming in contemporary society sometimes in spite of conventional stereotypes concerning men and women in evangelical communities. These stories are too often marginalized and deemed insignificant, inappropriate, or unwise by many evangelical leaders and communities. I would suggest, however, that objections against deep nonromantic transmarital relationships are rooted more in the romantic myth than in the created order.

Gender, Sexual Drive, and Order

Many Christians believe that the story of the first man and woman, Adam and Eve, presents us with a divinely-imposed order for male-female relationships and family. Some evangelicals read the Genesis narrative as providing a literal, once-and-for-all template for gender order in marriages, families, and communities. This sense of a prescription from God taken directly from the Genesis text has had far-reaching social ramifications for men and women. Author Leanne Payne reflects this kind of gendered order and its implications for women when she writes:

> Generally speaking, a woman, when happy to be herself, and not overly influenced by today's feminism and political correctness,

does not seek a cutting-edge public ministry. Rather, her gender drive with its strong desires lead her to seek a loving husband, children, and a home. Until fairly recent times, especially as a Christian, she valued the comparative "hiddenness" and needful protection that goes with such desires, knowing home and hearth to be her special sphere of greatest joy, influence, and effectiveness.[6]

This sounds more like the June Cleaver than the "model" woman described in Proverbs 31. Christians with longstanding, deep-seated beliefs like Payne's about "gender drive" have particular views of ordered relationships and intimacy in society. This traditional view of normative gender roles in homes and churches pushes many people into stories of conventional conformity when it comes to women and gender issues. Shame and psychoanalysis came against anyone deviating from the norm. In the 1950's, for example, women were urged to stay at home rather than work outside the home: "Even in her own limited realm, if a wife asserted an independent opinion over simple family or even personal bodily decisions, psychomedical experts often stood ready, along with husbands and fathers, to block her way."[7] Yet today, such women are viewed as courageous and even heroic.

Order and gender role have informed core family values in many communities. Martin Luther wrote, "A woman is not fully the master of herself. God fashioned her body so that she should be with a man, to have and rear children." In contrast to the husband who is the ruler of the house, "woman on the other hand, is like a nail driven into the wall."[8] Julie Ingersoll tells us in her book, *Evangelical Christian Women: War Stories in the Gender Battles*, how often women who feel called into ministry were "challenged as to why they were not home with their children."[9] In this traditional model, women are perceived as threatening the stability of the family if they form and nurture a transmarital, paired cross-gender friendship. Such actions would be unwise at best, and "un-Christian" at worst.

For many conservative believers, sexual drive towards the other sex is almost embraced as a nonnegotiable part of the created order. A number of Christians, like my former pastor (who told me I was playing with fire), believe men and women are hardwired for sex, as if that is the *sole* purpose for female-male relationality in Christ's kingdom and the world. It is "natural" and therefore predictable for men and women who enter into any kind of close relationship with each other to take it to the next and ultimate level—which would mean having sex. According to this interpretation, romantic and sexual coupling is in our genes as a man and a woman get close to one another, according to this interpretation.

With irresistible force, nature takes over and overrides the best of intentions between the sexes with irresistible force. Conversation, then, about male-female relations before marriage or in addition to marriage immediately goes toward temptation, lust, avoidance, rules, and boundaries. The discussion quickly degenerates into finding a list of rules to stave off powerful sexual urges. This common approach, however, is in danger of reading into the divine order a narrow, Freudian view of human nature as well as the romantic myth.

For centuries male-female friendship was a "natural" disorder according to philosophers. Men believed women were incapable of friendship. Plato, Aristotle, and Cicero all wrote treatises on the nature of friendship, and all three thought it was unnatural for women to participate in enduring, virtuous friendships. In the sixteenth century, Montaigne wrote that "the normal capacity of women is, in fact, unequal to the demands of that communion and intercourse on which the sacred bond [of friendship] is fed; their souls do not seem firm enough to bear the strain of so hard and lasting a tie."[10] One nineteenth-century novelist, Dinah Mulock Craik, comments on cross-sex friendships, "they are more rare to find, and not happiest always, when found; because in some degree they are contrary to nature."[11]

Fear of women, sexuality, and disorder between men and women in church history is well documented. Church fathers praised virgins, but according to Jane Tibbetts Schulenburg, they also saw the "female nature as fragile, weak, and in general, as participating in the carnal, as sexual, and thus incompatible with the spiritual world."[12] In some communities cross-sex friendships were seen as dangerous and a sign of social disorder. Caesarius of Arles for example, ordained as a Catholic bishop in 502 feared women and disorder in close friendships, including cross-sex relationships. He warned the people under his spiritual care that a man and a woman should not, "be allowed to speak together alone for more than a moment."[13] He predicted disastrous consequences for close cross-sex relationships: "Know most certainly that a woman who does not avoid a familiar relationship with men will rapidly destroy either herself or the other."[14] According to Gregory the Great, "men should love women as if they were sisters, but they must also flee from them as if they were one's enemies."[15] Theologian Jean Gerson (1363-1429) cautioned, "for even the most deeply religious men, no matter how great their sanctity, a common life and familiarity with women are not safe."[16]

It would be naïve if we assumed that the idea of intimacy leading to physical sex was considered problematic only between friends. The sex drive impacted all male-female relationships including brothers and sisters in some communities. Augustine would not allow his widowed sister to stay with him in the same house.[17] During the medieval period there were fears of priests impregnating their own sisters. Schulenburg reports that between the fifth and the ninth centuries, some faith communities began segregating brothers and sisters. They were not to sleep in the same room, and eventually, no female could live in the same house with a man—whether he was her brother, father, or close relative.[18]

Male-Female Intimacy and Nonromantic Order

Does the "true nature" of close male-female intimacy inherently lead to sex? Are men and women hardwired to fall into "something else?" Lisa Gee grounds her secular argument for intimate, nonromantic paired friendships between men and women in the historical and present reality of close, affectionate brother-sister pairs. Although some contemporary feminists tend to steer away from this family relationship metaphor, Gee believes it is the best model for passionate but equal friendships between men and women. She observes, "Brothers and sisters and opposite-sex friends develop, sustain and importantly—enjoy, extraordinarily deep, intimate relationships, rich in unfettered communication, relaxation and laughter."[19] Contemporary Christians rarely balk at or are suspicious of close, biological adult brother-sister relationships. Indeed, many don't think twice about a brother and sister spending time alone with each other, living alone with each other, or sharing physical affection. This has not always been the case.

From a Christian perspective, the complex brother-sister bond as a nonromantic model for male-female friendships holds great power and promise. Throughout antiquity, writes Reider Aasgaard, these relationships were characterized by "strong and positive emotions towards one another."[20] In many cultures, spanning thousands of years, adult brothers and sisters have loved each other deeply, passionately, and fiercely with no sex between them.

While there were medieval Christian communities which segregated brothers and sisters for fear of sexual intercourse, there were also monastic communities where brothers and sisters were permitted to enjoy their familial bonds without fear. Many sisters for example, helped their brothers establish monasteries. Schulenburg lists numerous dyadic relationships responsible for establishing monasteries during this time. There were brother-sister teams who traveled together alone on missionary journeys. These pairs expressed sweet affection towards each other. One leader frequently expressed his closeness to his sister: "He calls her, 'dearly beloved sister,' 'sister whom I love,' 'my comfort and solace,' 'shelter in Christ ... security,' as well as the 'better part of our body.'"[21] Schulenburg notes that in one tradition, a number of narratives "emphasize the special devotion and profound love between saintly brothers and sisters."[22]

At the one end of the spectrum, then, were faith communities enforcing strict boundaries between brothers and sisters for fear of incest. At the other end were communities in which brother-sister pairs were able to freely love each other without fear or censure. Perhaps the juxtaposition of these opposite reactions does provide a complex background for passionate nonromantic male-female relationships. As we saw in chapter two, Freud introduced a "natural eroticism" into all relationships but he maintained that it started in the home—including between brothers and sisters.[23] Ernest Jones, Freud's biographer and disciple, suggested that, "The characteristics of the father-daughter complex are also found in a similar one, the brother-sister complex."[24] Incest between brothers and sisters does happen, but it is the result of disorder, not of the natural order of the relationship. Gee suggests that, "Many brothers and sisters have deep, close relationships, very few ever have sex."[25]

Gee asks, "Why have we embraced a view of human nature which, at its most dumbed-down, figures us as a semi-repressed sex drive on legs?"[26] Is this the predominant story of sexual formation Christians want to tell in the twenty-first century? What stories of sexual formation are we telling people in our communities? In my thirty years of attending churches I have heard two narratives in Christian communities: 1) the marital/romantic story, and 2) the danger story. Both stories of course, involve an introduction, a plot, and a climax towards the same thing: sex. Freud no doubt, would heartily endorse these two stories. But are we to settle for only Freudian sexual formation in our faith communities? As Protestants, we have to ask ourselves, why do we reduce deep, male-female intimacy in our communities to the great Freudian "sex charade?" If the church is going to present an alternative, eschatological community of brothers and sisters bonded together as *one* in Christ, formation and friendship must suggest that Christian sexuality has *multiple* paths for men and women.

Where are the redemptive stories of nonromantic, intimate relationships between men and women in our evangelical culture? Perhaps the complex depth of the brother-sister metaphor in the Christian story can help us see that the deep, nonsexual male-female intimacy is a powerful third way between the two stories of romance and danger: "Whoever does the will of God is my brother and sister and mother" (Mark 3:35).

This metaphor suggests a different kind of nearness with the other sex—a *nonromantic* nearness. The relationship transcends sexual relations. Adult brothers and sisters may or may not end up living with each other, but their childhood experience under the same roof forges a different closeness with the other sex than romantic/sexual nearness. This is not necessarily an idealized nearness. It is a closeness that is vulnerable to all the potential and real complexities and difficulties of living in the same house: rivalry, jealousy, violence, ambivalence, and so on. This nearness of siblings does not produce an instantaneous or automatic positive devotion or bond with the other gender. It is a relational process of deepening trust and closeness. But brother-sister bonds throughout the centuries have produced deep loyalty, affection, and solid trust. Lisa Gee comments, "The intensity of love, the strength of the connection between brother and sister, can be equal to that between husband and wife, but … it is of a fundamentally different nature. The one need not preclude or even impede the other."[27]

The brother-sister relationship suggests a wide and deep emotional range for adult men and women. In many ancient cultures including Jesus' own, "the strongest ties were between brothers and sisters, not between husbands and wives."[28] It was not a given in Christ's time, that husbands and wives would be "romantic friends" as our culture expects. In fact, even after marriage, "Brothers remain their sister's primary source of 'companionship, advice, help, and defense." It was not uncommon for brother-sister relationships to have what we would consider to be a "romantic quality" about them even after one of them married.[29] Brothers and sisters were life-long companions, affectionate, with strong devotion to one another. Even in some contemporary cultures this strong tie between a brother-sister dyad is the norm. In the Trobriand Islands near Papua, New Guinea, "the most important woman in a man's life is his *sister* rather than his *wife*; and the most important man in a woman's life is her *brother* rather than her *husband*."[30]

Understanding the relational depth between brothers and sisters in the ancient world, we have a better glimpse of the lover in the Song of Songs: "You have ravished my heart, my sister, my bride, you have ravished my heart with a glance of your eyes, with one jewel of your necklace" (Song of Songs 4:9). By using the language of siblings, the Song of Songs is highlighting the exceptional intimacy and bond between these two lovers. Christian marriage should be the passionate union of brothers and sisters in Christ.

In healthy families, brothers and sisters grow in their knowledge of one another understanding that this relationship is sex-free. They do, however, have the opportunity to learn depths of nonsexual physical intimacy between the sexes: hugs, kisses, embraces, massages, playful tickling, and so on. Here is where it is possible to learn nonromantic touch and play with the other sex that shapes our view of intimacy. Lilian Calles Barger notes, "The abandoned disclosure of intimacy requires both emotional and bodily trust that what I place in your hands will not be refused but will be cared for, cherished, and valued."[31]

In the New Testament the brother-sister metaphor is another term for the sacred, deep, nonromantic nearness between men and women in the kingdom of God. The brother-sister metaphor also anticipates the embodied nearness between men and women for all eternity—and suggests we can experience some of that depth as we live between the already and the not yet. Alasdair MacIntyre writes, "I can only answer the question, 'What am I to do?' if I can answer the prior question 'Of what story or stories do I find myself a part?"[32] In the new heavens and earth, Jesus said something significant will change in marriage. "For in the resurrection they neither marry nor are given in marriage, but are like angels in heaven" (Matt.22:30).

Protestants have taken Jesus' meaning to be that there will be no sex in heaven. Some Church fathers saw virginity as the highest state of spiritual maturity. Christians do not agree about what this saying of Jesus means for men and women either in the age to come or for male-female relationships today. It does seem, however, to suggest that the powerful human mystery of embodied love will be present in some way that is not lessened between men and women. In contemporary language, Jesus is saying that our sexual scripts for paired relationships in the new heavens and earth will look different from the present sexual scripts. Laura Smit muses: "But in the next life, our capacity for love will be much greater and will grow throughout eternity. We simply do not know how this love will be expressed, though it will certainly be something that will make our current experiences of sexual intimacy seem pale and uninteresting."[33]

A Third Way of Sexual Formation in Male-Female Intimacy

The stories of Jesus and women are open to rich, diverse, positively constructed thinking about female-male relationality, boundaries, and friendship in the new creation. Despite the fact that some Christian communities have strongly objected to both same-sex and cross-sex friendships in order to avoid any hint of sexual immorality, others throughout the centuries have nurtured stories of nonromantic intimacy between men and women. In fact, while some enforced strict boundaries between men and women, other Christian men and women were empowered by Jesus' friendships with women to intentionally pursue close, paired female-male friendships. Their stories offer a compelling case for the rich relational depth between men and women. Unsurprisingly, these opposite approaches to cross-sex friendships also parallel how communities addressed brother-sister relationships.

Many in the evangelical sub-culture are virtually unaware of the deep friendships that have existed between men and women in the church. As a result, evangelicals have no place for stories beyond the romantic and danger narratives. Well-meaning Christians tend to use this silence to argue the wisdom of marginalizing paired cross-sex friendships for the protection of marriages. Thus, many in our contemporary churches do not know a powerful third way exists.

Any notion of the historical rarity of male-female friendship cannot be isolated from the larger narrative of a patriarchal Christianity. For the sake of the greater good of the kingdom, it is worth reconsidering that infrequency in light of the larger backdrop. Gender order and fear of women are pervasive in the patriarchal paradigm, and that includes male-female friendship. Jane Tibbets Schulenberg in her book *Forgetful of Their Sex* comments:

> Scholars have traditionally perceived "real" or "true" friendship as a singularly male experience. With few exceptions the myths about devoted friends, societal models of friendship, or treatises on friendship have been about men and for men. ...In their studies, historians, anthropologists, sociologists, philosophers and others have either failed to observe female friendships and cross-sex friendships, or have treated them as merely a peripheral part of the social system. Scholars have generally seen women as totally subsumed by their families and with little need or time for the cultivation of external bonds or friendship.[34]

Contrary to this emphasis, however, there is an impressive array of rich, close, cross-sex friendship stories, in spite of the many predictable social and religious barriers that have thwarted such social pairings. The complex ambivalence about men and women in spiritual friendships can be seen throughout church history in the juxtaposition of misogynist, sex-segregated attitudes with fully developed intimate male-female relationships. With respect to friendships, boundaries between Christian sexuality and spirituality shifted within communities as well as between them.

Wendy Wright observes that in the monastic tradition women formed enduring, lifelong close friendships with men. She notes, "It is indisputable that in the medieval world women often found a sphere of creativity and personal expression in the monastery that was unavailable to them elsewhere." She also bears witness to the fact that the medieval era had a "good number of male and female spiritual friendships whether women as individuals or as a group did or did not escape the denunciations flung at them."[35] Schulenburg also observes that the "bonds of friendship seem to have played an extraordinarily significant role in the lives of medieval women and men."[36] In some communities during the Middle Ages, deep, affectionate cross-sex relationships flourished. In more gender-inclusive communities, strong friendships could easily deepen given the close physical and spiritual proximity between men and women. Several of these narratives are well-known in Christian spirituality, especially in the Catholic tradition.

Jodi Bilinkoff argues that this third way of navigating intimacy, which avoids the extremes of sex-segregation and sexual relationships, was a powerful Catholic apologetic for converting women and encouraging them to stay in the community during the intense division with Protestants after the Reformation. This proved effective in the era when Catholic communities (as well as Protestant's) accused priests of preying upon women sexually. She observes, "Given this pervasive cultural stereotype, one might think that these descriptions of intense male-female relationships and the use of highly affective language would only fan the flames."[37] And they did. It was not that the fiery gossip had no substance to it— there were instances of seduction by priests. However, there were also priests who formed chaste, passionate friendships with women (including married women), and the written accounts of these would be passed on to other women who faced choices between a Catholic community and or a Protestant one. What made these friendships even more complex and unusual given the climate of patriarchal fear, the priests believed these women had direct access to God in a way they did not.

The Reformers rejected the practice of confession between priest and people. But as Bilinkoff reports, confession with a spiritual director opened the door to spiritual intimacy, a nonromantic nearness between the sexes. She shows Catholic confession during this time allowed women to be known, heard, respected, and intimately loved by men. Some of these women had a relational authority with these priests (because of the priest's assumption they had direct access to God) thereby creating an informal but nevertheless real authority in leadership. This was also in a period when husbands may or may not have offered relational intimacy to their wives—including sex, and in other Catholic communities where priests feared any kind of closeness with nuns. Written stories of deep friendships between priests and women became a Catholic apologetic during this religious civil war which emphasized fear of women, fear of sex, and fear of any kind of nearness between sexes. In the context of confession and spiritual direction, Bilinkoff notes that this "offered something that may have been quite rare for women in premodern society: sustained and serious conversation with a member of the opposite sex."[38] Given the fact that in some communities, even biological brothers and sisters were segregated, confession would offer the opportunity to form relationships between men which were not possible anywhere else in the family or neighborhood.

Fortunatus, St. Radegunde, and Agnes

Fortunatus was a monk in the sixth century who had two close women friends. He took up residence at a monastery and formed a close friendship with a woman, St. Radegunde, who was the founder and the spiritual leader in that community. While there, he also met Agnes, and a deep friendship ensued between them. Their closeness raised suspicions among others in the community, and Fortunatus assured Agnes that he had the same depth of feeling for her and no more than he had for his own sister. But he didn't back away from owning that it was nonetheless a passionate love. He wrote to Agnes:

> You, who, because of your dignity, are a mother to me and [who] are my sister by the privilege of friendship, you to whom I pay homage involving [all] my heart, faith and piety, whom I love with divine, entirely, spiritual affection, devoid of the guilty complicity of the flesh and senses, I call to witness Christ, the Apostles Peter and Paul, Saint Mary and her pious companions that I have looked at you with any other eye and with any other sentiment than if you had been my sister Tatiana, if our mother Radegunde had carried us both in her chaste flanks, and if her holy breasts had nourished us with her milk. I fear, alas! For I see danger in it, that the least insinuations of evil tongues repress the demonstration of my feelings.

However, I am resolved to live with you as I have done up to now,
if you are willing to continue our friendship.[39]

He wrote poems to both Radegunde and Agnes, calling Radegunde,
"mother," and Agnes, "sister." Their passionate friendships flourished in
this community until Radegunde died. At one point, there was serious
conversation between the three of them about being buried in a single
tomb together.

According to Alan Bray, in his book *The Friend*, male friends were
buried together in tomb monuments clearly on what was church property.
He reflects on the significance of male friendship and joint monuments
during this period. Are we surprised, as Christians, to find out there
were men and women friends who were buried together in tombs
with joint monuments on what was clearly church property? Herbert
Vaughn, a Catholic priest, and Lady Herbert of Lea formed a long-term
intimate friendship, and asked to be buried side-by-side.[40] These were
friendships, not marriages. But they were not casual relationships either.

St. Radegunde, in fact, was by no means the "weaker sex" or promiscuous
when it came to relating to men. She sought out and maintained
relationships with other men, including several bishops. She had a
close bond with St. Junien, the founder of a monastery in Maire. They
exchanged gifts and prayers. She was a leader who took initiative in
establishing a monastery and overseeing it. When St. Radegunde was
dying, she sent a messenger to Junien in order to see him before she
died. Meanwhile, Junien had sent his messenger to St. Radegunde with
a similar message. These messengers met somewhere in the middle of
their intended journey, and they both carried messages to inform close
friends that the other was dying. St. Radegunde and Junien died on the
same day, August 13, 587.[41]

St. Hathumoda and Agius

Although we don't know many of the details of medieval friendship
between Hathumoda and Agius, we do have a record of Agius' words to
those who gathered for Hathumoda's burial.

Believe me, you are not alone in this grief, I too am oppressed by it, I too am suffering, and I cannot sufficiently express to you how much I also have lost in her. You know full well how great was her love for me, and how she cherished me while she lived. You know how anxious she was to see me when she fell ill, with what gladness she received me, and how she spoke to me on her deathbed. The words she spoke at the last were truly elevating, and ever and anon she uttered my name.[42]

Queen St. Margaret of Scotland and Turgot

While Queen St. Margaret of Scotland (1046-93) was married to King Malcom III, she had a close friendship with her confessor, Turgot, bishop of St. Andrew. It is illuminating to learn that Christian leaders like Turgot formed friendships with women and inspired others to do the same. While some bishops urged high boundaries when it came to cross-sex friendships, other leaders like Turgot did not fear "the wind of temptation"[43] and practiced close friendships with women. In the eleventh century, for example, Bishop Azecho of Worms wrote a pastoral letter to the men and women under his spiritual care advocating warm, close, spiritual friendships between the sexes. He envisioned men and women who formed close friendships as brothers and sisters who were "cohabiting in God."[44]

Turgot and Margaret enjoyed one of the clearest examples of an intimate, transmarital friendship in the Middle Ages. Margaret married King Malcom III in 1070, and by all historical accounts they had a happy and successful marriage. They had six sons and two daughters. During their marriage of twenty-three years, Queen Margaret formed a close spiritual friendship with Turgot. After Margaret died, her children commissioned him, her confessor and companion, to write her biography. In this royal family of Scotland, a deep, spiritual, transmarital intimacy and a happy Christian marriage were not mutually exclusive.

Stories of intimate relationships between bishops and those under their spiritual care perhaps seem strange to the ears of many modern evangelical pastors and believers who see ministry and relationships in the model of the modern business/professional and sexual segregation paradigm. But even more stunning than a Christian leader seeking intimate friendships with those under his immediate oversight is a male leader seeking intimate friendship with a woman—a married woman. In his biography Turgot highlighted the Queen's love for books and its role in their friendship: "She had in fact great religious greed for holy volumes, and *her intimate friendship and friendly intimacy with me compelled me to exert myself very much in procuring them for her.*"[45] In another place he mentioned that Margaret bared the secrets of her heart to him in their ongoing friendship. He was with her for several days while she on the verge of death. She entrusted her youngest children to him as she received word shortly before she died that her husband had been killed just days earlier. Turgot gives a moving account of the mutual affection between Margaret and himself in the last hours of her life on earth. It is a story of two sacred unions: husband and wife, and wife and her close male friend. In her last hours, Turgot reports that Margaret began "to relate her life to me in order; and to pour out river of tears at every word ... while she wept, I wept also."[46]

Francis de Sales and Jane de Chantal

The term "friendship" doesn't even begin to adequately describe the fullness and depth of the relationship between Francis de Sales, the bishop of Geneva (1567-1622) and Jane de Chantal (1572-1641). If their friendship were the only cross-sex relationship from Christ up to the present day, it would unequivocally resolve the question, "Can men and women pursuing holiness enjoy close friendship with one another?" The eighteen-year friendship between Francis and Jane is probably the best known male-female friendship in Catholic spirituality even while their paired intimacy remains largely unknown among contemporary evangelicals. As Wendy Wright notes, "Between the years of 1604 and 1622 Francis de Sales and Jane de Chantal shared in a spiritual friendship of intense and mutual creativity."[47]

It would be an injustice to their relationship to either romanticize it or sexualize it. Francis lived a life of vowed celibacy. A vowed celibate is committed to purity, to a pure inner life, and to eliminating any lust in his/her imagination. Francis was *not* merely a single man. A single person is someone who is unmarried but is open to pursuing a romantic path if he/she is sexually attracted to a member of the other sex. Francis vowed never to pursue that path. Although some think celibacy must entail hatred of sex and fear of women, Kathleen Norris sees deep cross-sex friendships as a path of intimacy practiced by "people who are fully aware of themselves as sexual beings but who express their sexuality in a celibate way."[48]

Francis was a young bishop and Jane, a young widowed mother when they met in August of 1604. She was searching for a spiritual director. From their first encounter, they had a mutual sense that God had brought them together. Francis exercised caution in his writing on friendships. For him, friendships were the most dangerous of loves. It is striking to note given the fact that he was influenced by what was happening during this time: that while he had a number of friends including women, he never entered into any close relationship with a Protestant. Initially, after he met Jane, Wendy Wright suggests, he distanced himself emotionally and spiritually from Jane.[49] More than six weeks later, though, he would write to her, "God, it seems to me, has given me to you; I am more sure of it every hour."[50]

Sometimes trust in relationships takes time to form and cultivate. At other times, when individuals have a sense that it is of God, trust and bonding develop more rapidly. One of my cross-sex friendships began through an online group discussing theology. The first time my friend called our house, my wife answered the phone and gave her a warm greeting. When I spoke with her, we had a brief conversation and then I prayed for her. As she tells it, God met her through my prayer for her in a way she had not expected. She had a strong sense that God was working through our relationship and a deeper trust immediately began to form.

In spite of the deeply ingrained traditional concerns about the dangers of a celibate man and woman experiencing deep intimacy, Francis and Jane formed a passionate and deep friendship. Their passionate love for each other grew as they supported each other in their respective callings in God's kingdom. Francis wrote to her in October 1604, "This feeling I have for you has a certain particularity that consoles me no end, and to tell the truth, it is extremely profitable to me."[51]

Their friendship, like Jesus' friendship with women, can inspire us to not turn our backs on the compelling mystery and depth of male-female nonromantic closeness within the church and society. In observing their profound mutuality, Carole Hallundbaek writes:

> What is unique in the correspondence of Francis de Sales and Jane de Chantal is the degree of freedom of expression they enjoy with regard to the affection they feel for each other's person and journey. In this day of correct, even sterile, behavior between colleagues (especially in the church) in an increasingly litigious society, it is wonderful and refreshing to find two people who can express their love and affection for each other with such openness and freedom...[52]

Such freedom between friends, and most particularly between members of the family of God, should not be exceptional; if anything, it is essential. "Mutuality is the source and the gift. It is at the heart of creation, of life coming into being and giving back, again and again."[53]

Francis as a man and Jane as a woman communicated the language of love for each other in friendship. Henri Nouwen observed, "There was no holding back, no careful distance, no concern about possible misinterpretations, no fear for too much too soon. To the contrary, there is constant encouragement to be open, direct and spontaneous."[54] Their story is a positive example of spiritual friendship before the Freudian age when men and women both could express the language of emotional depth in their friendships without suspicion of sexual advances. It also reveals a language of closeness free from a culture of romanticism.

The friendship between Francis and Jane happened in a patriarchal era in which men were believed to be rational and women emotional, in which women were traditionally viewed as dangerous. Sex was one of the most dangerous things in the world to a soul vowed to celibacy. Yet they loved each other and were confident of communicating a *different* kind of deep love for each other. "I am inseparable," wrote Francis, "from your heart and, speaking with the words of the Holy Spirit, we now have only one heart and one soul, because I find that what is said of all the Christians of the early Church is, thanks to God, now true of us."[55]

Their language of love as friends is not an isolated incident. Resisting stereotypes at many levels, male and female friends in the Christian community before Freud mutually expressed their love for each other while remaining chaste in their relationships. Saint Ecgburg in a letter to her close friend, Saint Boniface, wrote, "As I acknowledge the bonds of your affection for me, my very inmost soul is filled with a sweetness as of honey."[56] In her letters to him she yearns for him. She asks him for a small token or some of his writings, "so that in them I shall always have your presence."[57] Her letters to him tell him how much "she loved and needed him."[58] In a context of people hungering for relationships that are characterized by God's passionate love, Dan Allender, founder of Mars Hill Graduate School, writes in his book, *Leading With A Limp*: "Imagine saying this to someone who is your friend: 'I miss you when we're apart. I'm so delighted when we're together.'"[59]

The language of love Francis shared with Jane was common in many cross-sex spiritual friendships in the Christian world before Freud and before the romantic myth. Even with the conventional perceived threat of sexual danger that existed in Christian communities for centuries, Francis could write to Jane: "God gave me a tremendous love for your soul. As you became more and more open with me, a marvelous obligation arose for my soul to love yours more and more."[60] It is not as though Francis or Jane were naïve about the seductive power of carnality in friendship. He counseled Christians to be cautious with and even avoid such relationships. Their language and passionate love certainly would have been considered "dangerous" or inappropriate between a man and woman in other communities influenced by patriarchal views. Yet over three hundred years later, Henri Nouwen has said their friendship model is "crucial for our own spiritual survival"[61] as Christian men and women living in the contemporary world.

These stories from the history of the church offer us something beyond the two extremes (the romantic and the danger stories) presented in many churches when it comes to male-female intimacy and rightly ordered relationships. They suggest there is something *much more* for men and women than segregation practiced by many Christian communities. Quite clearly, there are Christian men and women who have drunk deeply from the well of nonromantic, chaste, passionate friendship. They are not narratives of sexual promiscuity or sexual anxiety over language, behavior, or emotional depth. They do not present us men and women "caving in" or succumbing to irresistible impulses in their passionate love, nor do they convey calculated distance between men and women as friends. Their long-term, spiritual and emotional intensity surprises those of us unacquainted with these relationships. Such intensity in transmarital friendships is centered in passionate love with a commitment to the fidelity of marriage and friendship. These friendships are a different kind of sacred union, and they show us a third way of ordered relational love in the twenty-first century.

CHAPTER 4

SACRED UNIONS
AND FRIENDSHIP

"That they may all be one."

Jesus Christ

There is a rich relational and theological concept making a comeback in
Protestant circles. It has significant import for spirituality and interpersonal
relationships—including marriage. What is it? *Union.* Robert E. Webber
writes: "I don't doubt that for many spirituality as *union with God* is a
new insight. And that is because *union with God* has become lost in the
twentieth century."[1] Kevin Vanhoozer speaks of this union: "Christians
share a common Spirit—a Spirit whose work is precisely to foster union
and communion, to make *one*."[2] Scot McKnight suggests:

> Nothing in the Bible makes sense if one does not begin with the
> garden of Eden as a life of oneness—human beings in union with
> God and in communion with the self, with one another, and with
> the world around them. Life is about 'oneness'—oneness with God,
> with ourselves, with others, and with the world. When this oneness
> is lived out, God is glorified and humans delight in that glory.[3]

Contemporary Christian thinkers are beginning a new conversation
about what eschatological union can look like in the here-and-now.
Christians readily acknowledge the sacredness of marital union. In most

conservative communities "union" or "oneness" between a man and woman is almost always reserved for romantic or married couples. In the conservative scheme, male-female "unions" are romantic relationships. As we saw in previous chapters, there is a rich stream in other faith traditions regarding a different kind of union—a "two-in-one" intimacy in spiritual friendship reflecting the deep inner love of the Trinity. It is this eschatological union we are moving toward—our identity as *one* just as the Father and Son are one. While the union of spiritual friendship should not be restricted to marriage, it is all too often neglected even within marriage.

What do evangelical theologians mean when they state that life is about oneness? How do we as a church embrace a positive, constructive, authentic view of sexuality between all men and women in marriage and beyond marriage knowing that "when oneness is lived out, God is glorified and humans delight in that glory?" If McKnight's perspective is solid, shouldn't *all* Christian men and women desire, indeed, passionately desire oneness in their relationships? Shouldn't we desire oneness with the other sex beyond our spouse? Are singles called to desire oneness with members of the other sex in the kingdom? What, then, does communion between men and women look like in the kingdom of God? These questions take us deep into oneness, marriage, friendship, and community.

Rethinking Male-Female Oneness in the New Creation

In God's story, something dramatic happened in the incarnation, life, suffering, death, resurrection, and ascension of Jesus Christ:

"All this is from God, who reconciled us to himself through Christ, and has given us the ministry of reconciliation; that is, in Christ God was reconciling the world to himself, not counting their trespasses against them, and entrusting the message of reconciliation to us. So we are ambassadors for Christ, since God is making his appeal through us; we entreat you on behalf of Christ, be reconciled to God" (2 Corinthians 5: 18-20).

Christians, Paul Wadell reminds us, "believe the life of Jesus, and especially his death and resurrection, permanently changed the world." He adds that the infant church believed that Jesus inaugurated "a new age with new possibilities." Moreover, "Jesus' whole life showed that people do not have to be governed by fear and mistrust, by calculated self-interest, by defensiveness or insecurity."[4]

In this new age, as the New Testament makes clear, there are new social intimacies. God in Christ has made us his ambassadors of passionate reconciliation and peace. He has come to bring flourishing peace where hostility, ambivalence, fear, and mistrust have reigned among people. We must recognize the dramatic implications for male-female relations. The harsh realities of sexual brokenness between men and women confront us in the news, in therapy sessions, in confessions, in divorce courts, in our homes, and beyond. Yet Christ *is* reconciling sexuality and spirituality through his reign and he's doing it through men and women in wild, outside-of-the-box ways, as well as within simple, flawed but growing marriages. One of the forms this reconciliation of men and women, of sexuality and spirituality, can take is the communion of male-female friendship in Christ.

The Scripture provides twelve key themes that can help us understand how male-female intimacy in friendship is an expression of God's heart for deepening reconciliation between men and women in Christ. They include the husband-wife relationship but go beyond it.

First, man and woman each have been created in God's image. In Genesis 1:27 we read, "So God created humankind in his image, the image of God he created them; male and female he created them." There has been considerable discussion about what the image of God means, but one thing is clear: both man and woman share the likeness of God. There is profound oneness expressed in this text. Differences? Yes! But there is nevertheless an equal, profound union. There is no hierarchy between them in sharing God's likeness. James H. Olthuis writes, "Humanity is a male/female community of reciprocity, mutuality and co-creation ... men cannot be defined without reference to women, nor can women be defined without reference to men."[5]

Second, God created the husband-wife relationship in the garden of Eden. In the beginning God created male and female; he pronounced them "very good" (v.31). God delights as sexuality and spirituality come together in companionship, procreation, partnership, play, friendship, in marriage.

Third, there is the new order in Christ. Rosemary Rader in her book, *Breaking Boundaries*, suggests that early Christians saw "a new world taking shape."[6] In the old world, the surrounding patriarchal cultures had no place for nonsexual male-female relationships outside the home. But the New Testament writers encourage men and women to consider new social possibilities in the reign of Christ. The images of "new wine" (Mark 2:22), "new teaching" (Mark 1:27), "new covenant" (Luke 22:20), "new self" (Ephesians 4:24), "new Jerusalem" (Revelation 21:2), "new heaven and new earth" (Revelation 21:1), and "I am making all things new" (Revelation 21:5) stir new hope for a mature sexuality in Christ's kingdom. This new order is articulated by Paul in Galatians 3:28: "There is no longer Jew or Greek, there is no longer slave or free, there is no longer male or female; for all of you are one in Christ Jesus." Wendy Wright suggests Paul means "not in the sense that one's God-given sexuality is erased – but that the sexes are not necessarily divided against each other but rather gathered up together in their full distinctiveness and brought to God."[7]

Fourth, the brother-sister model we have already observed introduced new possibilities of a profound nonromantic nearness for believers. This close bonding between the sexes in non romantic contexts is readily visible in most cultures. Paul's admonition, then, for his readers to treat "younger women as sisters—with absolute purity" (1 Timothy 5:1) would actually encourage close, nonromantic relationships between men and women in the community. The brother-sister metaphor suggests the possibility of a deep intimacy between men and women who are not related to each to other within Christian community. "The church now constituted the Christian's family, with the odd result that complete strangers might be able to claim the most intimate relationship."[8]

Fifth, we have what could be called metaphors of intimacy emphasizing closeness, and deep attachment. As *men* and *women* together we are: "branches" (John 15:5), "one body" (1 Corinthians 12:13), "living stones" (2 Peter 2:5), a "royal priesthood" (2 Peter 2:9), and Christ's "bride" (Revelation 21:2). The striking thing about these images is that there is no hint of sex-segregation or social division of unmarried and married individuals. All these passages suggest a deep communal love between men and women within marriage, as well as communal, nonromantic male-female intimacy coexisting beyond marriage.

Sixth, consider all the "one another's"—none of which have a sex-segregated command embedded in them. Here are just a few: "welcome one another" (Romans 15:7), "pray for one another" (James 5:16), "be kind to one another" (Ephesians 4:32), "greet one another with a holy kiss" (1 Corinthians 16:20), "teach and admonish one another" (Colossians 3:16), and "confess your sins to one another" (James 5:16). None of these contains transcultural, sex-segregated warnings to keep men and women from meeting privately or in public, or from avoiding the powerful intimacy that may grow because male and female friends seek to be obedient to these commands in their nonromantic relationship.

Seventh, Lisa McMinn suggests God's abundance is grounds for cross-sex friendships extending outward from the marital relationship: "To live in abundance rather than scarcity is to explore and embrace the depth of love possible in an exclusive relationship, rather than to focus on the moral restraint that limits that kind of love to one other."[9] This reflects the extraordinary love of God. Abundance doesn't undermine exclusivity in marriage, but flows out of it. As Kenda Creasy Dean observes, "The God of Jesus Christ *does* love excessively, extravagantly, 'outside the lines.'"[10] And we are to be imitators of God in Christ. This is also tied to Christ's teaching that there will be no marriage in heaven. Many Christians have understood this teaching to mean that marriage will be fulfilled—marriage itself points to a much greater union.

Eighth, there is goodness in desire toward the other sex. Christian spirituality embraces and affirms desire, longing, and yearning. We're not Buddhists or Stoics. Solomon writes, "Some friends play at friendship but a true friend sticks closer than one's nearest kin" (Proverbs 18:24). The *New English Bible* translation puts it, "Some companions are good only for idle talk, but a friend may stick closer than a brother." Christian sociologist Dennis Hiebert states, "Attachment experienced as a powerful desire to be with the other is perhaps the most profound characteristic that separates the loving of friends from the liking of associates."[11] He adds, "Attachment with a cross-sex friend is not in and of itself, 'a subtle failure in fidelity.'"[12]

Stanley Grenz suggests that a mature sexuality makes an important distinction between sexual desire and desire for sex. He believes sexual desire "refers to the need we all share to experience wholeness and intimacy through relationships with others. It relates to the dimension often called *eros*, the human longing to possess and be possessed by the object's of one's desire." He suggests sexual desire encompasses a wide-ranging depth of human behaviors and desires; whereas desire for sex is, well, desire for sex! He writes, "For many people, the desire for sex, the longing to express one's sexuality through genital acts (*venus*), is psychologically inseparable from sexual desire. Nevertheless, for the development of true sexual maturity, a person must come to terms with the differences between these two dimensions and learn to separate them both in one's psychological state and in overt action."[13]

In other words, there is distinctive beauty and goodness present in a sexual desire which yearns for social oneness with the other sex and which cannot be categorized as possessive lust. Writing of transmarital cross-sex friendships, James Olthuis observes,

> Men and women do desire to relate to each other and become close. We do need and want to share intimacy and understanding. But for many of us this natural desire never has a chance to develop because we are haunted by the idea, common currency in our society, that being close always leads to the bedroom. That idea is simple, unadulterated nonsense.[14]

Ninth, we have the striking, breathtaking beauty of triune love. While we should heed the caution to avoid too much speculation about the inner life of the Father, Son, and the Spirit, it is virtually impossible to consider the oneness Christ prays for his people in John 17 and without imagining how it impacts mutual honor, love, and delight between men and women. Marva Dawn suggests, "Our trust in the Trinity's embrace frees us to love others more fully with triune kinds of love—fostering deep relationships that involve solid friendships without any sexual *innuendo*."[15] Paul Wadell highlights the nature of true love:

> In the divine friendship, the perfect outpouring of love between the Father, Son, and Spirit results in unbroken oneness and a community that is never diminished by rivalry, jealousy, or selfishness. In God we see a community in which persons are not set over against each other, but a community in which friends flourish through freely given love. In God we do not find a community fractured through struggle, conflict, and domination; rather we see a community in which differences of persons are celebrated, respected, and affirmed.[16]

Tenth, Scot McKnight highlights another theme reflecting the union between men and women: what did women do? He surveys both the Old and New Testaments asking this important question. Were they spiritual leaders? Yes, Miriam and Deborah were spiritual leaders. Presidential leaders? Yes, Deborah was "the president, the pope, and Rambo all bundled up in one female body!"[17] McKnight goes on to mention Junia, "the apostle above all other apostles," and Priscilla, who taught scripture and theology, and Phoebe, deaconess and benefactor.[18]

Eleventh, there are the masculine and feminine metaphors of God in Scripture. These call our attention to the richness, ambiguity, and mystery of being created in the image of the God. Many conservatives react with either nervousness or fear when female images of God are brought up. These images call our attention to the beauty of the triune community. Beauty, as David Bentley Hart reminds us, has a way of defying our carefully ordered and controlled distinctions:

For Christian thought, beauty's indifference to the due order of far and near, great and small, absent and present, spiritual and material should indicate the continuity of divine and created glory, the way the glory of heaven and earth truly declares and belongs to the glory of the infinite God.[19]

Deeper reflection is needed as more and more contemporary women connect with female images of God. These metaphors do not demand that we conceive of God as "simply a melding together of male and female spiritual essences,"[20] nor are we left with God as male or female. In fact, there are many metaphors in scripture depicting God as an inanimate object. We do not conclude, because biblical writers call God a "rock" that he is impersonal or not a living being. Kristina LaCelle-Peterson observes, "God encompasses all human characteristics but transcends both sexes."[21]

Last, but certainly not least, we have Jesus. We will look at stories about Jesus and women in depth in the next two chapters, but as an expression of God's overall deepening reconciliation, Jesus says: "I give you a new commandment, that you love one another. Just as I have loved you, you also should love one another" (John 13:34). He does not indicate the doers of this command should be sex-segregated. In light of Jesus' close friendships with women, this commandment strongly suggests robust possibilities for embodied male-female friendship—not just in the final age, but here and now in the kingdom under his reign.

These themes lead us to a robust richness in male-female oneness for the new reign of Christ in the present, as well as in the fullness of reconciliation in the new creation when Christ returns. A close look at them suggests a complex, multidimensional oneness in the body of Christ. Stanley Grenz comments:

Although marriage is the primal male-female relationship, the biblical narrative points to the eschatological new creation as the fullness of fellowship toward which human sexuality has been directed from the beginning.... The unity in diversity that arises out of the bond that brings male and female together in marriage offers an obvious picture of the unity and diversity present within the triune God. But it is not the only picture. Indeed, it is not the most significant picture.[22]

The husband-wife relationship doesn't cover the range of embodied oneness in this age or the next. In fact, it is not even the *ultimate* picture of union. Paul Wadell suggests that friends in Christ "will have much greater intimacy and unity between them than they would if they lived together but were united over a lesser good." He suggests, following Augustine, "the greatest possible intimacy comes not from physical closeness or even physical expression, but from belonging to the body of Christ."[23] Our union in Christ as men and women then, has profound implications for both married and unmarried individuals.

"The new intimacy," writes Christine Colón and Bonnie Field, "not only takes the place of marriage here on earth but also allows singles to participate joyfully even if they never received a spouse."[24] Our union with Christ in baptism opens the door for extraordinary, passionate intimacy in friendship: "The love that characterizes true friendship is precisely the kind of love that will be the bond of unity in the everlasting kingdom ... to pursue friendships in the beauty of holiness is to drink deeply of the mystery of God's kingdom."[25] These realities of new order in God's kingdom reflect a profound reordering of male-female relationships. In the Old Testament, the positive pictures of male-female love centered upon marriage and family. But in the New Testament, oneness is no longer solely for husband and wife, although "one flesh" remains an important union in Christ. There is now a complex social oneness between men and women in the body of Christ for the world to behold. Some evangelicals call this "sexual shalom." Judith Balswick and Jack Balswick in their book *Authentic Human Sexuality*, suggest the metaphors of love and closeness described in Isaiah picture shalom between men and women in the new heavens and new earth:

> The wolf shall live with the lamb, the leopard shall lie down with the kid, the calf and the lion and the fatling together, and a little child shall lead them. The cow and the bear shall graze, their young

shall lie down together; and the lion shall eat straw like the ox. The nursing child shall play over the hole of the asp, and the weaned child shall put its hand on the adder's den (Isaiah 11:6-8).

The reality of sexual shalom in Christ's new creation promises a deep and healthy wholeness—a wholeness of dwelling together side-by-side in close proximity, where the vulnerable (a lamb) will live with an aggressive predator (a wolf). This has implications for every man and woman in the church. Christ did not come merely to fix problems in struggling marriages or to address marital insecurities.

The sexual theology of our evangelical churches has been too small and defensive. For the most part, evangelical sexual theology has circled the wagons around marriage, with an inordinate focus on "one flesh," in hopes of saving this union as the one and only sacred union between men and women. In our defense of marriage, many of us have failed to notice the false boundaries erected by years of sexism and patriarchy in the church. The longstanding, pervasive stereotype depicting men as logical, rational, sexual beings in contrast with women as the emotional ones still lingers in the evangelical subculture and our broader society. For hundreds of years men have formulated rationalist theologies while deeply fearing passion, emotion, and mystical experience in spiritual and sexual formation. Lilian Calles Barger writes, "We can no longer accept male-centered assumptions nor be trapped by 'feminine' spiritual history. We need the whole range of knowledge and human experience to bring us to wisdom."[26]

In our fear of the fire in sexuality, we have erected false boundaries in the form of fixed roles and universal rules in marriage, friendship, and community—false boundaries of safety, romance, male-female intimacy, and even masculinity and femininity. However the bold, redemptive realities of kingdom sexuality speak of a radical oneness that is both broader and deeper than the Mars/Venus approach, or any other strident contemporary voices claiming one-size-fits-all solutions. On the one hand, we all know of cases where the slippery slope was pretty slippery for some, and they fell. On the other hand, there are plenty of real-life stories of innocent passion and intimacies between men and women in friendships that do not end in bed or distancing the other sex in a gender-based hierarchal order.

In my experience, it is rare to find evangelicals who are aware of the numerous male-female spiritual friendships in the Catholic tradition. But they are all too aware of stories of sexual brokenness, and they maintain a false boundary of one communal norm for all male-female intimacy outside of marriage. It would not be much of a stretch to say that modern evangelicals tend to fear the vast wholeness of sexual mystery and passion in the Christian tradition.

Reverence for Redemptive Intimacies

Although friendship has an elastic meaning that covers everything from two strangers with loose organizational affiliations to the most intimate relationship, there is a place in the Western world for reverence for our deepest friendships. Emerson wrote, "Friendship demands religious treatment.... Reverence is a great part of it."[27] He adds that when friendships are real, "they are not glass threads or frostwork, but the solidest thing we know."[28] Caroline Simon reflects on reverence in friendship and muses, "A friendship that calls for reverence is a relationship in which the friend is valued as irreplaceable, as one for whom, within one's circle of affection, there could be no double. In the most significant kind of friendship, we value our friends for their own sake, not just as pleasant company or as social assets."[29] Perhaps when we embrace a more robust, deeper understanding of Christian sexuality, oneness, and friendship, we may discover relationships embodying redemptive intimacy between men and women. In marriage we discover the goodness, beauty, and glory of another as God sees him or her; similarly, in friendship we discover the goodness, beauty and glory of another.

In each intimacy, the other person becomes irreplaceable and priceless. In the formation of oneness in friendship and/or marriage, two individuals "do not at the same time cease to remain two."[30] Reverence discovers, discerns, and distinguishes the expansiveness of otherness and intimacy.

Reverential intimacy means that we rethink old stereotypes, preconceived ideas, fears, and false boundaries of safety. In this context reverence is not something stodgy or driven by a fear that never takes chances or risks. Oneness in sexuality and friendship calls us to sacred unions both in marriage and beyond marriage while deeply respecting different kinds of "irreplaceable" friends and unions.

Sexuality and Friendship in Marriage

Nobody who genuinely loves his or her spouse has any idea on their wedding night of getting a divorce anytime in the future. Sadly, the statistics bear witness to the fact that one of out every three will get divorced before they are married ten years. One might say that an individual comes to see his or her spouse as replaceable. The ironic but striking reality is that many married couples do not forge a significant spiritual friendship. It is even more ironic when we consider that our whole culture holds up romantic friendship as the highest of all human relationships.

In addition to this, the phenomenon in many universities known as "hooking up" is an approach to sexuality and friendship with profound implications on sexual formation. Although the reasons for marital breakdowns are complex, the culture of hooking up is shaping how young adults see sexuality, friendship, and marriage. The hookup system, as Kathleen Bogle reports, tends to favor men: "For those on the outside looking in, it may appear that men and women are on an equal playing field in the hookup culture on campus. Upon closer inspection, however, it becomes clear that college men are in a position of power.... While the hookup system works for men, it does not provide a good way for women to get what *they* want."[31]

The formation of spiritual friendship within marriage ought to be a goal for all Christian communities to have for all marriages. It provides a kingdom alternative to the over-romanticizing of marriage, and the glorification of orgasm as the ultimate end of communion. In practicing mutual spiritual friendship, husbands and wives are disciplined to discover a fidelity to each other that surpasses their fidelity to the institution of marriage itself. Friendship forges a communion apart from the sexual objectification of women (or men for that matter), while also fostering mutual equality through confession, forgiveness, prayer, delight, play, trust, and a common vision for a missional purpose beyond their own relationship. Even a cursory glance at spiritual male-female friendships from the past reveals that the friend had a powerful bond based on drawing out the best in each other. When passionate communion does not revolve around sex or narrow gender roles, both men and women flourish in love.

Friendship between the sexes as an expression of Christian sexuality celebrates a delight and appropriate desire in the other's beauty and goodness—a beauty deeper than fixation on sex or sexual objectification.

In other words, there is a sexual beauty in both sexes which is far deeper and more attractive than what our pop culture tells us is attractive and sexy. In his insightful, secular book, *The Centerfold Syndrome*, Gary Brook explains the complications entailed when young men grow up with an image of sexual attractiveness that equates with only a tiny percentage of women. "An unattractive partner (a 'hound') was a disgrace. It may have been marginally acceptable to briefly or covertly date a hound for sexual exploitation, but extended contacts made a guy a target for public ridicule." On the other hand, young men could not trust the "gorgeous" women, for "we expected them to be the target of every horny guy in the world."[32]

As Brook points out, when the particular form of a woman's body is objectified (in the popular culture this is always young, slim, woman without blemish) young men attempt to "score" with the hottest girl. This uncritical adoration toward what Brook calls "trophyism" creates an unhealthy dissatisfaction among men, since women's bodies (even the great looking ones) age and are vulnerable to changing circumstances. He writes that men "have been encouraged to glorify the objective physical aspects of women. We have been taught to compete with each other, with women's body as prizes.... We have been allowed to seek comfort and nurturance from women's bodies, but conditioned to restrict our awareness to only our sexual needs."[33]

Cultivating virtues that enable us to have a holistic vision of beauty and goodness in the other in spiritual friendship is not trivial for today's men and women. The cultivation and practice of spiritual friendship between husband and wife is a deeper, passionate alternative to the shallow, immature romantic relationships glorified by our pop culture and perpetuating false boundaries of intimacy, shallow beauty, and the objectification of women. The roots of sacred union in marriage go deep into the beauty of life-giving authentic oneness between the sexes. And there are stories of chaste but intimate friendships in which both the man and the woman have opened themselves to the sexual mystery of communion, but not sex.

This strikes at the core of sexual formation for spiritual friendship in marriage. In our culture, the perception is: men want sex while women want friendship or intimacy. A sexual formation that seeks the wholeness of both worlds would strengthen marriages. Contemporary authors Douglas Rosenau and Michael Sytsma observe: "It is possible to learn the skills of enjoying the opposite sex without zooming in on erotic interaction and to take delight in the distinctive beauty of others without wanting to consume or possess it (them). In popular culture there often is an over-emphasis on erotic sexuality at the expense or neglect of the whole dimension of gender sexuality. This is true for both single and married individuals." They add, "God is the ultimate father and we are all brothers and sisters, enjoying each other in His sexual world."[34]

Reverence between husband and wife maintains a respect for the uniqueness of the other and a healthy separateness from the other. David Benner suggests that the emphasis on the one-flesh metaphor so prominent in books and sermons about marriage should not mean a fusion of the two spouses in which one or both lose their individual identity. Furthermore, a reverence for our spouse's uniqueness means we celebrate the reality that he or she is not the same as I am. We are to prize and nurture our spouse's uniqueness in our marital friendship.[35]

But it doesn't end there. Spiritual friendship in marriage cherishes the fullness of the sexual bond between husband and wife. Sex is not just sex. Sex is not just using the parts and plumbing to form the glue for a functional, cooperative partnership outside the bedroom. In Christian sexuality and spirituality, marriage is not merely spiritual friendship plus sex. We must not underestimate or undervalue the fire and powerful energy of sex as a passionate, maturing expression of oneness in marriage. There is a sexual knowing in marriage which transcends friendship between sexes outside of marriage. Acts of sex are not the sole difference the between deep friendship of spouses and the deep friendship between an unmarried man and woman. Spiritual friendships between husband and wife and between those who are not married to each other have the same goals toward reconciliation and love in Christ: oneness, intimacy, beauty, fidelity, and union. But these are *different* sacred unions.

Since conservative Christian leaders have had such a difficult time sorting out what sexuality and friendship look like even within marriage, they have sent confusing messages to their communities. Many Christians throughout history would not have affirmed the goodness and beauty of sexual pleasure in marriage—sex was only for procreation. And we are still wrestling with the concept of holistic goodness of genital pleasure today. Carmen Renee Berry quotes a friend who is a pastor: "I was taught two contradictory things about sex. First, it's dirty. Second, I should save it for the one I love."[36] Many well-intentioned parents communicate a message of shame or ambivalence about sex to their children. Jack and Judith Balswick write that the message some parents their children is confusing: "The genital area is either considered nonexistent (something to be ignored or avoided) or bad (something disgusting)."[37] Contrast this to Catholic scholar Christine Gudorf's memory of hearing her father's Christmas toast to her mother at a family dinner when she was a young girl: "To Lucie, and her multiple orgasms."[38]

It is common knowledge that the Old Testament authors use a form of the verb "to know" to indicate sex or genital knowledge (Genesis 4:1, 17, 25; 1 Samuel 1:19). Many in the contemporary church are beginning to validate the richness, wonder, and beauty of genital knowledge in marriage. This has not always been the case. For historical perspective, it is important to note the well-known fact that many church authorities greatly feared the deeper waters of genital knowledge. It is commonly held that Augustine had a negative view of sexuality. During the early part of the Middle Ages, some Roman Catholic churches enforced strong guidelines for marital sex. According to Elizabeth Dreyer, "Married couples were permitted to have intercourse only a few times a year."[39] Even to this day, Christians wrestle with deep ambivalence about dualistic attitudes toward sex. Dreyer observes, "The inferior status assigned to the body and 'erotic' passions has been particularly onerous for women, with whom these qualities are culturally associated."[40] Lewis B. Smedes starts off his book, *Sex for Christians* observing "The toughest problem Christians have with sex is how to feel about their own sexuality."[41] For so long, genital knowing and pleasure were linked with the flesh, lust, and carnal desires. Desire for sex was not a good desire—even in marriage.

A husband and wife enter into marriage with solid public vows to protect an "us" in major and minor conflicts. These vows of fidelity have never consisted of one universal norm for marital relationships across all cultures and time. In our own society these vows might be: to give pleasure to each other in sex and tender affection; to actively pursue forgiveness and reconciliation in small and large hurts; to mutually seek each other's greatest potential and gifts; to be there for each other in the face of financial hardship and/or blessing, chronic illnesses, families of origin, friendships, and aging bodies. Starry-eyed romanticism has faltered for many couples, in both the church and in the world. But there is a rootedness to marital and sexual fidelity that goes beyond rules, cultural fads, and all other relationships.

With spiritual friendship in marriage, good authentic sex creates mutual pleasure, companionship, delightful play, and rooted intimacy.

Gudorf believes, "Sexual loving is central to marriage. The friendship and commitment of marriage is conveyed in sexual form." She adds, "The more pleasurable the sex—the more deeply satisfying it is—the more it sows the seeds for other goods in the marital relationship .... One of the tasks of the church should be to help make marital sex more pleasurable."[42] If both husband and wife seek to be generous in pleasuring each other, it can and does create a desire for more beauty and goodness in sexual intimacy. There is a richness and mystery to mutual sexual pleasure if we open ourselves, our fears, our feelings, our hungers, our passion, our entire selves to our spouses. This is not only true of newlyweds, but of enduring marriages as well. In sexual play, there is a vocabulary—a language—and a deep sense of trust that forms sexuality and friendship in marriage that cannot be duplicated in other male-female friendships. There is a social and private identity as a married couple. For twenty-eight years of marriage, Sheila and I have had our own sexual language. If either one of us attempted to use our vocabulary with someone else, it wouldn't make sense, for that language came into being in the context of our sexual intimacy and fidelity. It is engraved into our sexual identity as a couple. It is uniquely ours. God has a splendid and wonderful way of making all things new, including our sexual speech as a couple. It is our story.

In spiritual friendship, sexual play is initiated by either spouse over the course of a maturing marriage. Gudorf comments, "The assumption of dominant/subordinate relations is especially inappropriate in the area of marital sex.... The couple that feels that men should initiate and control sex will have a narrower sexual repertoire." Obviously if one gender (that is, the husband) is running the show, the creativity, passion, and spontaneity for arousal, foreplay, and orgasm doesn't come from a mutual trust and initiative, but only from the husband's limited perspective, creativity, and curiosity. Gudorf rightly points out, "Over a lifetime they will miss the many lovemaking sessions that she could have and would have initiated, either by letting him know that she was interested or by taking the initiative and arousing him to willingness to sexual play."[43]

Also, sexual play is just as important as mutual orgasms. It's not just about getting to the heat of passion. Sex is play. It is not about performance and not necessarily about a hot time every time. It is laughter, grace, sweetness, risk, and sometimes prolonged sessions of mutual pleasure and delight. Sheila and I have had many hilarious, gut-splitting laughs over our sexual play, and after twenty-eight years we are still enjoying sexual generosity between us with much pleasure.

Sexuality in Christian marriage declares sex between husband and wife to be more than just an intense friendship with fringe benefits. It is also more than just spiritual friendship plus sex: "The power and the mystery, and, therefore, the strength of the bond come from exclusivity.... What goes on between them is a profound mystery. The mystery of the mingling of souls."[44] Beautiful, pleasurable, maturing sex deepens the marital bond and companionship and is an icon for mystery and love. "Sexual joy is a picture of God's union with his bride."[45] This joy lingers and settles into the fabric of marital intimacy. It is not necessarily about the euphoria of one event. It is about inner sexual knowledge and trust.

Does this sexual mystery of exclusivity, though, in the larger context of the Christian story, *complete* bonding, connection, companionship, and friendship between the male and female? The romantic myth narrative strongly advocates an unequivocal yes. However, as we have already seen, Scripture suggests the partners in the sacred union of marriage are called to a robust, inclusive, far-reaching, widening circle of oneness in the body of Christ. This rooted, maturing singleness of heart in sexual fidelity expands our hearts to love our ever-widening circle of brothers and sisters in Christ, including our cross-sex friends. Here is where the richness of other metaphors and language, encompassing the oneness of Christ between men and women who dwell together in marriage, friendship, and community, enlarges our understanding of the already-but-not-yet tension in marriage. Christian marriage is not a call to an exclusive "couple's club"[46] of the two.

Here again, the exclusive boundaries of the inner nature of triune love call us to shape the ordering and mutuality between male and female in the new creation. There is a tension between exclusivity and inclusivity in marriage. Edith Humphrey reminds us, "Intimacy becomes possible because God is love, sharing intimacy within the Persons of the Trinity, and because God *delights also to move out to us*—to 'stand outside' the Godhead ecstatically" (emphasis added).[47] Or, consider a similar thought from Kenda Creasy Dean: "The *perichoresis* (literally, the 'dancing around') of the Trinity creates a unifying momentum that holds the differentiated persons of God together as one—distinct while in utter unity, passionately related to each other while ecstatically reaching out to humankind."[48]

Gordon Hilsman reminds us of the classic story of falling in love. In romantic love, when two individuals fall in love with each other, they see the distinctive elegance, beauty, glory, dignity, and profound specialness of what separates the other from billions. This knowledge, as it begins to take shape, may propel a man and woman into marriage. But the Christian story shapes this knowledge, as we are enabled, enlightened, and empowered to see others *outside* the exclusive relationship of marriage as distinctive sexual beings with profound dignity and beauty as well.[49] Elizabeth Dreyer says the triune community calls us as men and women to discern the "pseudo-beauty" of the world and the profound beauty of the other in friendship and community beyond marriage. "As we grow in our sensitivity to beauty," she writes, "we get a tiny glimpse of who God might be, for God is Beauty and Pleasure." She adds that, "When life involves noticing and responding to the vulnerable, needy, yet beautiful lives of others, it becomes a joyful existence.... Embracing the beauty of the world's mystery and unexplained depths is cause for rejoicing."[50]

Divine beauty then, calls men and women into a deeper reflection of the ways triune love shapes the beauty of sexual mystery in the present world. Some Christian thinkers call us to stop compartmentalizing and splitting eros and agape. David Bentley Hart suggests that the love to which God calls all Christians "is eros and agape at once."[51] This love, he states, is "a desire for the other that delights in the distance of otherness." James K. A. Smith observes that we are all "erotic creatures—that agapē is rightly ordered *eros*."[52] Seen in this light, eros between men and women in marriage and beyond it in *friendship* is not necessarily a synonym for lust. Our failure to apprehend this important distinction as Christians severely limits our response to the true and special beauty of our spouses and the beauty of those outside of marriage. John Navone writes, "The most intense delight of the saints, illuminated by Beauty Itself, will be to see God. In light of Beauty Itself we shall see ourselves as we are seen: the image of God. We shall know ourselves as we are known: the brothers and sisters of Christ."[53]

Sally B. Purvis observes how some Christian feminists see the flow of passionate agape outward from our marriage and immediate family: "If we expand our understanding of the energy and deep interestedness of passion, then the work of Christian agape is to make that passion more broadly available and more widely felt. *The task is not to curb passion, but to nourish it and channel it*" (italics added).[54] She adds further:

> If we understand *agape* to be intense, caring, passionate, other-directed, and respectful of the specificity of the beloved, then we can envision the normative flow of our individual and communal lives as ever-widening circles of *agape....* [T]he relationships in which we care most deeply and love most strongly, do not encompass the range of our obligation to love, but rather serve as guides and models for the movement outward into concern for all human beings.[55]

Sexuality, Oneness, and Transmarital Friendship

What about spiritual cross-sex friendships beyond marriage? The huge trend of women working outside the home, and the ability for men and women to engage each other on the Internet, have created wide-open social opportunities for men and women to become close friends. The question is not whether men and women can be friends; that is a question for other worldviews. Plus, strictly platonic, casual, friendly relationships are quite common in modern society. No, the question is, how do men and women created in the image of God nurture and delight in this deep interconnectedness they share in Christ? Love, the unbreakable, mutual, passionate, community of triune love called us into being. It is our identity as men and women. We were created and redeemed by Lovers and we are lovers. Marva Dawn suggests that "the New Testament language is lavish with words for love that help us build and revel in strong relationships of social sexuality with other members of our church or other communities."[56]

Joan Chittister, although writing in the context of female friendship, points us in the right direction: "Friendship is, in the end, always and everywhere eternal mystery, eternal desires. It is a grasp at the ultimate, the quest for human understanding."[57] Marriage is not the only male-female relationship which reveals the profound mystery and love of the triune God. The cluster of themes we looked at earlier in this chapter strongly indicates the formation of a deep, nonromantic, sexual mystery between men and women without having to have sex. Carmen Caltagirone (alongside many others in the Christian tradition) writes, "In intimacy the medium of exchange does not have to be sexual intercourse.... We must never limit it to romance; it is much more. We carry with us a part of those with whom we have entered into intimacy."[58] Although many are changing, conservative evangelicals still encourage false boundaries between men and women as wise and protective norms for all male-female relationships—in both leadership and the community at large.

These boundaries are false in the sense that they prescribe universal norms for faith communities which relegate all sexual mystery (if there is any left) to the marital bed. They do promote a sacredness and reverence for sexual union—and if they ignore women's initiative, passion, and leadership both in the bed and outside of it, they miss the feminine voice and mutuality. In this way, they are protecting only one romantic version of sexual union. In so doing, they downplay the depth of intimacy and passionate love in spiritual cross-sex friendship.

When the husband-wife model is exalted as the only relationship where passionate oneness occurs, we have set up false boundaries of safety, romance, and male-female intimacy. Anne E. Carr observes the profound depth that friendship offers: "A friend is one whose presence is joy, ever-deepening relationship and love, ever available in direct address, in communion and presence. A friend is one who remains fundamentally a mystery, inexhaustible, never fully known, always surprising. Yet a friend is familiar, comforting at home. A friend is one who urges human freedom and autonomy in decision, yet one who is present in the community of interdependence."[59]

From the Catholic tradition, Vincent Genovesi suggests, "When we act as loving individuals, we are acting as sexual beings, but we are not necessarily involved genitally." He adds, "What this means is that there is a whole other dimension to human sexuality, one that may be called the social or affective dimension, which shows itself in the human capacity to relate to others with emotional warmth, deep compassion, and tender affection. *All of these human qualities are rooted in sexuality and are true expressions of it, but they are not specifically genital in nature or focus*" (italics added).[60]

Genovesi argues a third way of sexual formation: interpersonal intimacy and true love can be experienced without sex or romance. He observes, "It is possible to live fully, healthfully, and happily without genital sexuality."[61] Perhaps more than ever, the sweeping changes in society call Christians to reconsider the vast richness and intimacy available in male-female relationships beyond the romantic myth. Putting it quite simply, Genovesi observes: "Experience proves that achieving oneness and intimacy is quite possible without genital expression."[62] The romantic myth wants us to believe that this is not true—that happiness, well-being, and the "life of oneness" can't be ours without romance. While there is a profound sexual oneness that is available in marriage, there is a broader oneness available to believers encompassing the depth of communion. As noted in chapter three, there is a great cloud of witnesses spanning the centuries to support the life-giving intimacy that happens in the sexual mystery of friendship.

Evangelicals have struggled with validating and positively embracing the promise of sex on the one hand, and promoting a dangerous message about sex on the other. As long as they maintain this posture, there is very little room the practice of the third way of deep intimacy or conversation. Hence, we have cordoned off sexuality into a "parts and plumbing" focus for romantic relationships with rigid boundaries which strongly discourage intimacy in cross-sex transmarital friendships. Since we can't imagine a lion being able to lay down with a calf, (Isaiah 11:6) conservatives discourage all nonromantic male-female closeness, physical tenderness, and sweet language of the heart.

Ruth Hudson expresses the fears of those who want to zealously keep all emotional and spiritual depth, passion, or intensity between men and women inside the romantic relationship. She writes:

> Most people underestimate the danger of close friendships with members of the opposite sex, because they start out innocently, and in the early stages, no sex involved. Very often, the person involved in this type of friendship does not realize how much of a threat it can be to his or her marriage or relationship.... If cultivated and nurtured over a period of weeks, months, and years, an innocent friendship between close friends of the opposite sex can escalate into an extramarital affair.... Today's opposite sex friendship can quickly become tomorrow's extramarital affair. Friendships with members of the opposite sex need to be monitored very closely, and checks and balances need to be put in place. Otherwise they can quickly cross the line.[63]

These are the very reasons some Christians fear embracing or nurturing passionate love and affection between men and women who are not in a romantic relationship. We settle for *a*sexualizing all male-female relationships outside of marriage. Does all passionate love in friendship and nonromantic physical intimacy undermine or threaten marital fidelity? What if cross-sex friends fully honored and supported marital fidelity?

While thousands of married Christian women would see passionate intimacy, long conversations, generous physical affection between their husbands and another woman as taking away energy and passion from their marriages, they themselves practice and engage in deep, often intense closeness with their female friends. Female friendships are known for their intense and passionate nature. If one listens to evangelical women prioritizing the marital bond, there tends to be universal agreement the marriage takes relational precedence over all other relationships. What does that really mean, though?

Many Christian women in our culture believe that they need an outside friend with whom they transparently bare their soul, their secrets. In many cases they share *feelings they can't discuss with their husbands*. In fact, in many marriages the emotional bonding between husbands and wives is *inferior* to that of the wives' friendships with women outside the marriage. This would constitute emotional adultery according to some definitions, because one spouse's heart is drawn away with so much energy and transparency spent outside the marriage. Irene Levine writes, "Many women are inseparable from their best friends: attached at the hip, talking to each other multiple times during the day—sharing confidences about their bodily secretions or fears of exposing their bodies in a bathing suit—things they would hesitate to share with their lovers."[64]

In *Frontline Women*, a married woman on the foreign mission field writes, "How I long for a consistent and long-term soul mate." Donna Downes, who quoted this woman (and is married herself) immediately responds, "This longing for intimacy and close friendship on the mission field characterizes both single and *married women*, the older and younger, the veteran as well as the newer missionary" (emphasis added). Then she adds, "Even if happily married, missionary wives still need close female friendships, realizing there is something special in the friendships of other women." So, at some level, even if there is deep intimacy between husband and wife, there still remains a deep yearning for companionship outside marriage because of the awareness of "something special" between women. In referring to the lack of intimacy within marriage, Downes quotes a veteran missionary, "Face it, men just don't often listen to us the way we need. Much as I deeply love my husband, often we're just on different wave lengths."[65]

Consider what was entirely acceptable for female friendships during the 1800s. One woman expresses her feelings about her lifelong friend: "To me it seems to have been a closer union than that of most marriages."[66] Sharon Marcus comments on the acceptance of both exclusive marital love and passionate friendships beyond marriage during the nineteenth century: "Marriage thus involved a singular and exclusive form of love, but it was also understood to include and even aspire to the love proper to friendship. Deeply religious women wrote of marriage and friendship as analogous relationships, both based on shared faith and both under-stood as ultimately a bond with God." She adds, "For those who took seriously the doctrine 'We are all one in Christ,' the concrete differences between spouses and friends became less significant."[67]

Deep friendships beyond marriages have also played a role for the other gender in Christian tradition. Puritan John Winthrop writes a letter to his friend, William Spring:

> I loved you truly before I could think that you took any notice of me: but now I embrace you and rest in your love and delight to solace my first thoughts in these sweet affections of so dear a friend. The apprehension of your love and worth together hath overcome my heart and removed the veil of modesty, that I must needs tell you, my soul is knit to you as the soul of Jonathan to David.[68]

History is filled with deep friendships coexisting with marriage. What if there is a healthy place in the kingdom for a happy marriage partner to enjoy the gift of passionate friendship with someone of the other sex? What if the yearning for deep friendships beyond marriage is a yearning for deeper communion beyond marriage? Fresh and deeper discernment is needed much more than simplistic rules or formulas drawn from black-and-white gender schemes about friendship and marriage. The idealistic romantic myth model falls far short of trinitarian love in a holistic Christian marriage and friendship. While the Christian story is clear that we live in a broken world, Stanley Grenz says, "maleness and femaleness impels persons to come together in many relationships that characterize human community."[69]

Engaging the Sexual Mystery

We have allowed the popular culture and the romantic industry to define delight and desire in narrow and reductionistic terms. Perhaps one of the greatest causes of discontented singles, struggling marriages, and rampant divorce in the Christian community is our narrow, awkward responses to these shaping influences. This is where Catholic and Eastern Orthodox spiritualities differ from much evangelical spirituality. There are streams within each of those traditions which usher saints into union with God and each other. Eastern Orthodox theologian Paul O'Callaghan writes, "The full intensity of love, commitment, devotion, and inner unity that typify the best of friends is an initiation into the communion that all will experience in Christ in the everlasting kingdom."[70] Within Orthodox spirituality, in relationships with spouses or closest friends, James Payton writes "we find fulfillment not in intellectual comprehension but in love which cannot be explained and beggars our words."[71] In other words, both deep friendships and marriages are, in their senses, unions; *both* are a foretaste of heaven.

Many evangelical communities are so intentional about forming *a*sexual friendships outside of marriage that there is little room for sexual mystery in friendship; there is room for only rules, boundaries, and fear. In *a*sexualizing friendship, we have left virtually no freedom to understand the depth of the idea that "maleness aches for femaleness, femaleness for the male,"[72] We believe we weren't made for that, or we must stay safely within the romantic ghetto of male-female relating and language. What we need is a sexual formation that will shape desire and delight on the grounds of the mystery of triune love and joy, instead of the nontrinitarian artificiality in pop culture. It could be that in our evangelical subculture we have so focused on the correct details of our doctrine of the Trinity, that we have shaped communities with little thought to the joy, beauty, and delight of the Trinity. Ruth Haley Barton observes: "There is no reason to think that men and women cannot forge friendships in which they become precious and irreplaceable to each other just as friends of the same sex do."[73]

Dennis Hiebert observes, "Sexuality is not merely some impulse contained in a safe-box to be let out only on special, appropriate occasions. Humans are not sexual only when they participate in sexual acts, and asexual at all other times."[74] Our embodied sexual selves, our sexual knowledge, and our sexual imaginations cannot be contained, confined, or captured in activities behind closed doors or sequestered solely into a romantic box. "Sexuality," writes Doug Rosenau and Michael Todd Wilson, "describes *who we are* more than what we do."[75]

It is this *true* love, beauty, and sexual mystery for which we are all wired. Friendship between the sexes in the twenty-first century summons us to a passionate reverence of the sexual knowledge and mystery we experience in redemptive intimacies with the opposite sex. Sexual mystery presents us with these powerful alternatives. At one end of the spectrum are inauthentic, indulgent, and immoral sexual "relationships." These relationships are marked by promiscuity, harassment, stalking, incest, adultery, date rape, hooking-up, and sexual power games in marriages, to name just a few aberrations. At the other end of the spectrum are relationships graced with tenderness, partnership, transparency, freedom, adventure, risk, mutuality, delight, fidelity, and physical affection.

The creative tension of sexual mystery in the Christian story invites us to the feast within marriage *and* friendship. The mystery invites us to a dance beyond our current range of language and whatever abilities we have to categorize or quantify. In a very real sense, God calls us to be sexual mystics. There is a deep ambiguity to sexuality and male-female intimacy that cannot be contained within the husband-wife relationship. As more and more cross-sex friendships become common in the twenty-first century, these two loves of marriage and transmarital friendship blending together but still respecting the differences in sacred unions can witness to a greater and yet more mysterious love: the eternal dance and delight of the Trinity.

Another aspect of the creative tension of this sexual mystery is the language of love in friendship between men and women. History reveals the sweet language of nonromantic nearness between brother-sister pairs and between cross-sex friends. There is abundant evidence of men and women using the intimate language of love prior to Freud and the introduction of the romantic myth. A robust sexual mystery calls us to return to the language of beautiful love and affection between men and women. We need to get past the awkwardness of expressing love, delight, pleasure, and goodness to each other.

This mystery summons us to a dance of creative tension beyond platonic relationship in which a man or woman never engages the other with their embodied selves. Yet the tension is there because there is no full, physical intimacy between friends. In marriage the fullness of physical, emotional, and spiritual communion is the dance. In friendship, both the man and woman reverently honor each other within the ordered limitations of friendship. But a triune kind of friendship dance in sexual mystery still provides an ever-deepening, ever-expanding range of intellectual, relational, and physical possibilities and experiences. Language becomes totally inadequate to describe the depth of our cross-sex friendship. Our friend is not our spouse. He or she is not our lover (being either spouse or lover communicates deep, mysterious relational possibilities). But in this dance our cross-sex friend is not "just" our friend, either. He or she is more than a friend. If both friends are open to be transformed and formed in their relationship, they enter that extraordinary, robust, passionate life of oneness in friendship and community.

CHAPTER 5

SACRED PASSIONS AND FRIENDSHIP

"Do not cling to me."
Jesus to Mary Magdalene in the Garden

In the beginning of the new creation, at the dawning of the new age with his resurrection, Jesus met Mary Magdalene, an unmarried woman, alone in a garden. A garden. The fact that Jesus would first appear to a woman with no else present at this pivotal moment in the Christian story would raise many questions for some about his relationship to her and the twelve male disciples. Nevertheless, Jesus saw Mary alone in a garden. John clearly put the empty tomb in the garden: "Now there was a garden in the place where he was crucified, and in the garden there was a new tomb in which no one had ever been laid" (John 19:41).

David Carr notes, "In the world of the Bible, gardens (and vineyards) are places where lovers meet to make love. At the same time, gardens often symbolize women and female sexuality."[1] The potential for scandal is so great that contemporary Christian authors Erwin and Rebecca Lutzer attempt to subdue the impact of this volatile rendezvous by stating, "This is the only time in the New Testament that Jesus and Mary Magdalene were alone together."[2] Certainly, we do not have another *recorded* incident, but this is like saying intimate friends only met *one*

ני

time with no one else present in a lavish honeymoon suite. If he would have appeared to both men and women in a group, it would have been read as a resounding triumph to champions of community. Similarly, if Jesus had chosen to meet either John or Peter, it would have been emphasized by all those who read divine design behind the male-first superiority in male-female relationships—echoes of a patriarchal reading of Genesis 1 and 2. At the very least, Jesus ignites our imagination concerning Christian spirituality and male-female oneness in the new creation. What is Jesus trying to convey by spending time here alone with Mary before appearing to anyone else?

If there is such a thing as a Christian spirituality of male-female friendship, it is unfolding before our very eyes in the garden with Jesus and Mary Magdalene—between human and divine love, between a male and female friend, between grace and nature, between heaven and earth, and on the first day of the new Creation, no less, empowered by fresh winds of resurrection, Jesus desired to meet Mary. Perhaps it might be considered premature at this place in the narrative to speak of a Christian spirituality between men and women, but in John's gospel, in particular, male-female sexuality and friendship seem to stand out as having a special emphasis.

Beyond his relationship with Mary Magdalene, John specifically mentioned that Jesus had a particular (indeed, preferential) love for Martha and Mary (John 11:5). This is striking because in the social world of Jesus' immediate context, and extending to the Greco-Roman world, men didn't think women were capable of friendship. Although the term "friend" was never used explicitly to define Jesus' relationship with Mary Magdalene, she was his disciple (John 15:12-15), and the term reflects Jesus' special and particular affection for Mary. His friendship with Mary takes on extra significance when he appeared to her in the garden. Although Mary is only mentioned once prior to the crucifixion, Jesus' choice to reveal his resurrected self to Mary, before meeting Peter, before...John, and before...other male and female followers puts male-female friendship right at the center of Christianity's pivotal moment.

This opens up the possibility for an entirely different script for male-female friendship within the new creation that God has birthed in Christ. Before we consider this specific type of friendship love between Jesus and Mary, it may be helpful to look back to the two most well-known friendships in the Bible.

Love and Friendship in Biblical Friendship Stories

Fasten your seatbelts. Fond as we Western Christians are of keeping eros, passion, affection, longing, hunger, beauty, and sexuality *out* of paired friendship-intimacy and contained only *in* marriage or romantic relationships, the stories within the biblical narrative itself tend to unravel our assumptions when they are closely examined. There are no neatly defined boundaries when it comes to the love between David and Jonathan. The first thing we read about Jonathan and David is that Jonathan's soul is "bound" to David's. The language of love and communion connecting Jonathan and David is much of the same language we find in the Song of Songs: "On my bed by night I sought him whom my *soul loves*" (Song of Song 3:1; 1:7, 3:2 emphasis added) with "As soon as he had finished speaking to Saul, the *soul* of Jonathan was knit to the *soul* of David, and Jonathan *loved* him as his own *soul*" (1 Samuel 18:1 emphasis added).

The garden language of soul and passionate love for lovers in the Song of Songs is the same language used for the friendship love between Jonathan and David. The same word is used in the immediate context of passionate *romantic* devotion later in the same chapter when we read, "Now Saul's daughter Michal *loved* David" (1 Sam. 18: 20). The term is used for other female-male couples. Issac loved Rebekah. Jacob loved Rachel. Samson loved Delilah. King Ahasuerus loved Esther. Elqanah loved his wife, Hannah. Although some commentators believe the love between Jonathan and David was merely a covenantal or political love, the language and the story of their love between them begs for a deeper understanding. In Deuteronomy 13:6 in the King James Version, we read, "If your brother, the son of your mother, your son or your daughter, or your friend who is as your own soul, secretly entices you, saying, 'Let us go and serve other gods,' which you have not known, neither you nor your fathers…" In biblical language, the bond of love between David and Jonathan is the language of inseparable union between two individuals in its deepest sense. Although the marital bond in Genesis 2 is described as "one flesh," the grammar of love describing David and Jonathan's friendship in 1 Samuel 18:1-2, is as if these two friends emerged as a communion of one. They were distinct and separate, yet their friendship is characterized as the deepest union possible.

Not only did Jonathan love David, but he "*delighted* much in David" (19:1), which again has linguistic links to the Song of Songs (2:7, 3:5, 8:4). This language of delight or desire is used to describe Jonathan's love for David *after* David married Michal. Susan Ackerman suggests, "Jonathan's emotional commitment to David … might be understood as eroticized in nature."[3] She points out that although delight is used in other passages to describe the intensity of one's feelings for gold, houses, and vineyards, it "figures in important ways in passages concerned with sexual desire and love."[4] She notes, "In Esther 2:14 for example, King Ahasuerus of Persia is said to send for a particular woman from his harem a second time only if she 'delighted' him on the first occasion, which is to say only if he has found sexual pleasure with her."[5] Ackerman suggests, "Together, these and other data allow for and may even promote the possibility of an eroticized and sexualized interpretation of Jonathan's feelings for David."[6] Must that really be the case? Before we delve into that, we must look at David's lament at Jonathan's death.

"I am distressed for you, my brother Jonathan; greatly beloved were you to me; your love to me was wonderful, passing the love of women" (1 Samuel 1:26). In chapter two we saw how the sexualization of passion and intimacy in modern relationships drove a wedge between friendship and warm, deep, passionate tenderness/devotion. Given these modern cultural assumptions, we are left with only two readings of the love between David and Jonathan: either it was homoerotic or it was strictly platonic in the modern sense of friendship. To be sure, many Christians who accept these conventions simplistically place all passion in erotic or romantic categories assuming God's created order. In so doing, what separates a modern healthy Christian marriage and close friendship in the minds of many is passion—intense feelings, devotion, affection. Platonic detachment is the healthy, appropriate norm for all friendships; romantic, sexual passion is considered healthy and appropriate only in marriage; passionate love cannot exist in friendship.

Sociologist Robert Brain speaks of this passionate nature of their love when he writes, "Jonathan 'fell in love' with David at first sight and his love never abated."[7] He comments, "These elements of friendship— loyalty, union, even passion—are found in other well-known myths of friendship."[8] He talks about his experience living in the Bangwa culture where "to have a friend was as important as having a wife or brother."[9] He describes the intensity, passion, and love he witnessed in these friendships including verbal and physical affection. Yet he was convinced, too, that their friendships were devoid of sexual love.

Could it be that modern Christian friendships resemble a detached view more in line with a Buddhist worldview than with God's own story? For Buddhists, distance from desire is a virtue. Non-attachment is highly esteemed. It is interesting to observe the absence of deep friendship when it comes to evangelical ecclesiology. In Jim Belcher's recent book, *Deep Church*, there is no chapter on friendship. In another book, *The Community of the Word: Toward an Evangelical Ecclesiology*, fourteen essays are included from different leaders, yet, deep friendship isn't discussed here, either. As we saw in chapter two, for centuries prior to Freud and the romantic myth, the story of love between David and Jonathan encouraged passionate oneness in friendships without sex. Friendship scholars have unearthed stories of passionate love in paired friendships in every century prior to Freud—including cross-sex dyads. If one suggests genital intimacy as the necessary natural path for this kind of emotional intensity between friends, we risk sexualizing and reducing all passionate love in relationships (same-sex or cross-sex) to only one outcome—like Freud did and the romantic myth does.

The biblical language of love in the story of David and Jonathan unapologetically describes it as one of the most profound forms of social relationship one can experience on earth. Paul O'Callaghan suggests that this story teaches us that "friendship can engender an intensity that stimulates the highest achievements of loyalty and devotion possible for human beings."[10]

If we listen with a careful ear to the stories in the Bible and in tradition prior to the twentieth century, we discover these stories inspired a deep, passionate language, devotion, and desire between friends from one generation to the next. As we saw in our discussion of the romantic myth, there were deep friendships (cross-sex or same-sex) expressed with intimate language long before the Victorian era. As Richard Godbeer observes for early Americans, friends had "an expansive and eloquent rhetorical space for the expression of same-sex love that was physically affectionate and yet nonerotic." In fact, he sees that "heroic and biblical precedents of love between men proved far more important than dark associations with sodomy as reference points for male friendship."[11]

Likewise, if we listen to stories of cross-sex *friendship* even before the nineteenth century, we find the similar language of depth, tenderness, devotion, and passion. Adam, a Cistercian monk (1198-1221) wrote to his friend, Agnes, "In my own way, most beloved, I wholly cling to you, and on your soul, mine depends. In this joining of individuals, the love of Christ has made itself our bond."[12] Jordon of Saxony (1190-1237), to his friend, Diana, wrote, "Within our hearts is the ardour of love in the Lord whereby you speak to me and I to you continuously in those wordless outpourings of charity which no tongue can express nor letter contain."[13] Jodi Bilinkoff, in her study of medieval male-female spiritual friendships, comments, "it is difficult to avoid being struck by the powerful and eroticized language used by these celibate Catholics."[14]

Many friendship scholars identify the cluster of European psychologists (most notably, Richard von Krafft-Ebing, Havelock Ellis, and Sigmund Freud) during the late 1800s as driving the modern wedge between friendship language and romance. Passion, intensity, and intimacy became sexualized—and so did language. Sandy Sheehy, writing on the impact this had on female friendships, observes, "Suddenly, what had seemed innocent, even exalted, became tagged as unhealthy. Experiencing intense feelings of affection, yearning for another woman's company, exchanging tokens of sentiment, articulating commitment, even providing comforting embraces in times of sorrow became suspect." Because of this sexualization of intimacy, "open physical affection between women began to seem dangerous, likely to arouse 'unnatural desires.'"[15]

The uninhibited language, devotion, love, and passion within the story of David and Jonathan just does not fit with modern friendship because Freud and the romantic myth have shaped moderns to be open to see such passion only in sexual relationships. Therefore, it is "inappropriate" in the Freudian sense. Scripture and centuries of numerous stories lead us to believe something different than detached, platonic, distant modern friendship. These stories reveal nonsexual, nonromantic sacred unions in God's story—including the grammar to inspire us.

The other well-known friendship story in the Old Testament is between Ruth and Naomi. The story introduces them as mother-in-law and daughter-in-law. Naomi's husband dies, and, ten years later, her two sons die leaving Naomi with just two daughters-in-law, Ruth and Orpah. The love between Ruth and Naomi in ancient history is a witness against the belief women did not have the capacity to form friendships of virtue as men did. After Naomi decided to return to her native land, she faces a difficult future without husband or sons. Ruth is no longer bound to Naomi by family ties. Naomi told Ruth to return to her mother's house. In response, Ruth declared to Naomi, "Do not urge me to leave you or to return from following you. For where you go I will go, and where you lodge I will lodge. Your people shall be my people, and your God my God. Where you die I will die, and there I will be buried" (Ruth 1:16).

These words have often been romanticized in Western weddings as a promise for marriage. Joseph Epstein reminds us of the irony of such use: "This verse, said by a friend to a friend, is nowadays mostly used in marriage ceremonies and is thought to represent the commitment that successfully flows from romantic love."[16] This verse has striking implications for Westerners who see friendship as a noncommittal relationship with no future expectations or obligations. What may be even more startling for contemporary readers who see friendship and marriage in black-and-white categories is the language of "clinging" in this friendship love. The narrator of this love story tells us that "Ruth clung to her" (Ruth 1:14). The word "clung" is the same term we find in Genesis 2 for relationship between a husband and wife: "Therefore a man shall leave his father and his mother and *hold fast* to his wife, and they shall become one flesh" (Gen. 2:24). Judith Kates and Gail Twersky Reimer write: "The word signifying Ruth's determination to stay with Naomi, 'clung' (*davka*), astounds us in the biblical context because it suggests a permanent attachment."[17]

This friendship story between two women speaks of a deep intentional bonding. When Ruth marries Boaz and gives birth, there is Naomi clearly in the center of what is happening in this family: "Then Naomi took the child and laid him in her bosom, and became his nurse" (Ruth 4:16). Their day-to-day attachment to each other did not end when Ruth and Boaz married. Contemporary evangelicals tend to put tremendous weight on the word "clings" in Genesis 2:24 to indicate emotional and relational separation from family and friends. However, the modern marriage model constructed by many evangelicals stresses the husband-and-wife as a stand-alone, "self-sufficient" pair. As we saw in chapter two, this notion is rooted more in romantic myth than in biblical values concerning intimacy. In this ancient story, we read of Naomi's continuing presence in the heart of everyday family life. Ruth's vow to her friend did not terminate when she took spoke vows with Boaz.

Within the Christian story there is the depth and richness of *troth* in friendship. Dan Allender reminds us that *troth* is an old term that meant "pledge of fidelity."[18] Naomi did not disappear into the outer fringes of Ruth and Boaz's marriage and family life. Friendship fidelity prior to marriage is honored, respected, and cherished within marital vows. Enduring friendships were not set in contrast to marital vows. In our modern romantic myth scripts, "She's just a friend" conveys a distance from vows, commitments, passion—a peripheral existence to the heart of the family. However, the bond between Naomi and Ruth did not drift away or become marginalized when Ruth married. The friendship stories of David and Jonathan and Ruth and Naomi provide a significant background for the particular friendship between Jesus and Mary Magdalene.

Sacred Passion Between Jesus and Mary

One of the most intriguing possibilities emerging in the story between Jesus and Mary is the notion of deep friendship, the yearning to be in the presence of the other:

> Early on the first day of the week, while it was still dark, Mary Magdalene came to the tomb and saw that the stone had been removed from the tomb. So she ran and went to Simon Peter and the other disciple, the one whom Jesus loved, and said to them, "They have taken the Lord out of the tomb, and we do not know where they have laid him." Then Peter and the other disciple set out and went towards the tomb. The two were running together, but the other disciple outran Peter and reached the tomb first. He bent down to look in and saw the linen wrappings lying there, but he did not go in. Then Simon Peter came, following him, and went into the tomb. He saw the linen wrappings lying there, and the cloth that had been on Jesus' head, not lying with the linen wrappings but rolled up in a place by itself. Then the other disciple, who reached the tomb first, also went in, and he saw and believed; for as yet they did not understand the scripture, that he must rise from the dead. Then the disciples returned to their homes. But Mary stood weeping outside the tomb. As she wept, she bent over to look into the tomb (John 20:1-11).

David Carr suggests, "John 20 simply depicts a woman desperately seeking the Lord she loves, willing to go to any lengths to find him, asking anyone she meets if they know where he is ... This text focuses on intense longing, though not specifically sexual desire"[19] It is her friendship with Jesus that causes her yearning to find Jesus, not the passion for sex or for romance. Jesus desires to meet her. She is longing for the Lord. This has the sense of an "innocent" but bold, uninhibited move that did not at all fit the gender norms of their immediate religious culture and surroundings.

The Gospels never give any evidence that Jesus married. As a matter of fact, despite speculations in popular culture on this side (*The Da Vinci Code*, etc.), there is no evidence that Jesus was married to Mary Magdalene or to anyone else. Jesus himself indicated that in the resurrection, men and women "neither marry nor are given in marriage, but are like angels in heaven," (Matt.22:30). Although we do not know if that means there will be sexual intercourse, it would at least seem to mean that males and females will relate to each other in the resurrection in a fullness of love and glory beyond marriage. Laura Smit suggests that: "It seems likely in the new creation we will find our capacity for enjoying one another, for seeing the glory in one another and delighting in it, expanded."[20] While it is not preposterous to entertain the notion that Jesus may have married, the fact remains that moderns assume, this side of Freud, that one can't live a vibrant life and passionate love in their sexuality unless one is enjoying sexual/romantic passion.

The story continues. As it unfolds before our eyes, there is no question Jesus desired to see Mary and *only her* before he saw anyone else after he was raised from the dead. Personal friendship and desire must be included as one of the mysterious divine reasons Jesus had for meeting this particular female disciple at the dawn of the new creation:

> But Mary stood weeping outside the tomb. As she wept, she bent over to look into the tomb; and she saw two angels in white, sitting where the body of Jesus had been lying, one at the head and the other at the feet. They said to her, "Woman, why are you weeping?"

She said to them, "They have taken away my Lord, and I do not know where they have laid him." When she had said this, she turned round and saw Jesus standing there, but she did not know that it was Jesus. Jesus said to her, "Woman, why are you weeping? For whom are you looking?" Supposing him to be the gardener, she said to him, "Sir, if you have carried him away, tell me where you have laid him, and I will take him away." Jesus said to her, "Mary!" She turned and said to him in Hebrew, "Rabbouni!" (which means Teacher) (John 20:11-16).

The meeting between Jesus and Mary Magdalene alone in the garden does not seem to be a meeting between romantic lovers. Can we prove it was not? No, we cannot subject this pair to a battery of pheromone tests and/or relationship quizzes to prove they weren't romantic lovers (thank God!). But the Gospels never give us any indication Jesus and Mary are the biblical version of Romeo and Juliet. His meeting with Mary (and only Mary) at this most significant moment in redemptive history has great import for sexuality and friendship in the kingdom. Elizabeth Moltmann-Wendel believes "a special intimacy between Mary Magdalene and Jesus can be inferred from the New Testament."[21] In the context of male-female friendships Catholic scholar Wendy Wright observes: "there is something unique about a way a man and woman are drawn toward another ... there is a power and deep wisdom to be discerned in the male and female dance of mutual desire."[22]

Contemporary theologian Paul Wadell, while not specifically tying this desire to male-female friendships, observes what others in the past have expressed about desire in friendship: "Love's desire is for the lover to be united with the lover. We want to be one with the people we love, not just close to them but intimately connected with them."[23] We see that kind of friendship-intimacy desire between Jesus and Mary in this story. Mary reaches out and embraces Jesus. Unlike the other disciples, Mary finds Jesus and holds onto him. Here, in the garden, there is a friendship love as "strong as death," (Song of Songs 8:6). F. Scott Spencer insightfully draws the link in passionate touch between Mary searching for Jesus and the Shulammite of the Song of Songs:

> Understandably, Mary wants to reinforce her personal talk with
> sensual touch, recalling the Shulammite who rose in the middle
> of the night to seek her lover and hold him tight: I will seek him
> whom my soul loves. *I sought him but found him not.* The sentinels
> found me, as they went about in the city. *Have you seen him whom
> my soul loves?* Scarcely had I passed them, when I found him
> whom my soul loves. *I held him tight and would not let him go....*
> (Song of Song 3:2-4).[24]

What if Jesus' desire to respond to Mary's longing with his immediate,
direct, embodied presence in the garden alone conveys the depth of
passion between them but without sex? It does challenge popular
assumptions about love, friendship, and male-female sexuality in
Western Christianity, where the church, for the most part, has allowed
the popular culture and the romantic myth to confine passion to sex.
Those who believe Jesus and Mary married cannot be content with
passion, sexuality, and friendship in the garden. They believe that all
passionate male-female sexuality must end in the bed. On the other
hand, it also disturbs those who have sexual assumptions about what
male-female sexuality *ought* to look like in communion between friends.
The former believe friendship accompanied by sexuality must end in
the sexual union of marriage. The latter believes a sacred union in
marriage must not open itself to any other kinds close male-female
intimacy beyond marriage. They both believe Genesis Chapters 1 and 2
narrowly define male-female sexuality prior to Christ's second coming.
What if cross-sex *communion* with a full range of nongenital passion is
realistically possible and accessible in the new creation without violating
the marriage bed?

Maybe sex didn't get in the way between Jesus and Mary in the sacred
events of the Christian story. What if Jesus' desire to meet personally
with Mary (that is, not just any random, abstract "woman"), instead of
his male disciples, or the community, gives us a glimpse of male-female
sexuality, a glimpse of the *new* communal mystery in the new heavens

and the new earth? What if Jesus didn't have an I-want-to-get-you-into-bed attraction or an infatuated attraction that turned into a compulsive meeting between him and Mary?

In John 19:38 and 20:11, we read of two drastically different reactions to Jesus from two different individuals, one male and the other female. Joseph of Arimathea, we are told, was a secret disciple of Jesus. He was afraid of the Jews and went behind the scenes to ask Pilate for Jesus' body. Meanwhile, fourteen verses later, we read that Mary, who had stayed visibly near to Jesus in life and death, was weeping at the empty tomb of Jesus. Wendy M. Wright, a Catholic scholar, reflecting on the bonding of genuine love writes:

> For love is not just a feeling or a transient emotion that sways one, nor is it simply a bracing tonic that sustains one for the struggle. It is a permanent if unseen force, a power stronger than death and greater than hell. In the slow and painful construction of genuine God-centered love, the fragments of a new reality are gathered up from amid all the brokenness, isolation, and estrangement of our lives.[25]

In healing Mary Magdalene, Jesus awakened love in her. This was not the distant, calculated kind of love. She opened herself to love this particular man. She was drawn into his passion for people, for life, for God; yet it was not a genital or romantic passion. He was intense. She was intense. She had never met anyone like him. She kept following him while other followers walked away. His messages divided people, yet she saw unmistakable love in him. Then he was crucified. She was compelled to be near him even as others mocked him on the cross. Her love for this particular *man* is not calculating but risky in the hostile atmosphere at the foot of the cross. "Passion fires the heart to love in many ways... Fear and cowardice close doors to intensity and commitment. It *is* dangerous to live passionately, and some may mistake fanaticism for true passion."[26]

"Abide in me," Jesus had told his disciples (John 15:4). In John's gospel, "abide" is a "verb with staying power."[27] Mary's devotion to Jesus to remain with him all the way to the cross and reminds us of Ruth's loyalty to Naomi. Once Jesus' love touched her, she stayed with him wherever he went. Perhaps she risked her life following him. When the Jews picked up stones to stone Jesus, she was near. It flew in the face of the communal Jewish wisdom to choose be near him, but she abided out of love. She was fiercely loyal. We all yearn for such love. She took the art of "being there" seriously. On the morning of the third day after his death, Jesus appeared to Mary in a garden.

Although Mary Magdalene is mentioned only fourteen times in the Gospels, the only woman mentioned more often is Mary of Nazareth. In John's gospel, Mary Magdalene is the only one weeping at his death. Moltmann-Wendel is among those who see the Gospels and the later Gnostic tradition as portraying Mary as an intimate friend of Jesus: "Mary Magdalene is the closest companion of Jesus, even if she did not kiss his mouth, but his feet."[28] When Jesus called her name (20:16), this marks the only time in John's gospel Jesus addressed a woman by her name.

There was more happening in this scene than just the affirmative value of a woman becoming the first witness to the resurrected Christ. Yes, in the resurrection, women are no longer the invisible sex. It is that, but it is much more than that. When Christ met Mary in the garden, friendship—not marriage, not family, not community, but male-female friendship—was the first relationship highlighted and attended to by the risen Christ at the dawn of the new creation according to John. Andy Crouch in his thought-provoking book, *Culture Making: Rediscovering our Creative Calling* suggests, "Jesus was a cultivator of culture." He "did not just teach creatively; he lived creatively, and the guardians of the horizons were unsettled by him." Jesus changed the horizons of all male-female relationships. "Friendship is a passionate connection that does not require sexual connection."[30] At this moment of the eschatological clock, there was "the creative passion for the possible."[31] In every generation since, the cultural and redemptive good of male-female friendship breaks forth as a passionate form of creative possibility countering the old, unredeemed ways of male-female relating.

Church tradition has often interpreted Jesus' command to Mary, "Do not cling to me!" (John 20:17) as the opposite of tenderness, of closeness, of warmth, of passion between men and women. Jane Schaberg notes, "The narrative is wide open to being read as centered on Jesus' rebuff of the touch of Mary Magdalene, correcting her and illustrating her stupidity, obsession, physicality, unseemliness, inferiority, and lust."[32] She reports that many church fathers used this verse as their apologetic for keeping women from teaching and administering the sacraments.[33]

Yet, many theologians are rethinking this longstanding assumption which has reinforced male-female stereotypes and distance in friendship and ministry. Some are saying Jesus' statement clearly presupposes they have touched before. Celia Allison Hahn, expresses, "To me the conclusion seems inescapable that she was in the habit of giving her friend a hug. Here, as in the intimate picture of the feet washing with tears and hair (Mark 14:3-9), is a portrait of a warm friend who accepted emotional and physical closeness with comfort."[34] While some have taken Jesus to mean, *do not think about touching me*, others see room for Mary touching and embracing Jesus, holding onto Jesus in passionate embrace—to which Jesus responds, "Do not cling to me." Even evangelical scholar Darrel Bock suggests, "She was clinging to Him so that Jesus told her to let him go."[35] There are no time markers indicating Mary was hugging Jesus for ten, thirty, sixty, or ninety seconds—we just do not know. But in a garden, this does recall the passion expressed in the Song of Songs: "When I found him whom my soul loves, I held him, and would not let him go" (Song of Songs 3:4). Mary was the first disciple to see Jesus, talk with him, touch him, embrace him. All the other disciples had scattered. "The words are not as harsh as they may at first sound. Jesus does not prohibit Mary from 'touching' him (see John 20:27), but from 'holding on' or 'clinging' to him."[36]

In the Songs of Songs, female sexual passion is celebrated rather than vilified.[37] Similarly, "Mary's passion here," writes Carr, "is no model of inappropriate eros. Her passionate longing is her greatest strength in this story."[38] Still, Jesus' words have a sudden shock to them, and Mary must have felt the ambiguity of the moment. Suddenly, Jesus "resists Mary's advances in a strikingly abrupt emotional swing."[39] Moltmann-Wendel observes, "No longer the tender, friendly Jesus. It is no longer possible to touch or anoint his body. He cannot be brought back and held fast."[40] Questions abound. They abound because of the way Christ embodied love and physical passion before his death. Earlier, he received the lavished physical affection of a woman repeatedly kissing his feet (no mere polite peck on the cheek). Jesus also allowed the male disciple for whom he had a particular and special affection for to lay his head on Jesus' chest (John 13:23). As Wisdom incarnate, Jesus was not afraid of sensual or passionate, yet nonromantic, physical affection with women or men. Carr suggests, "the Bible offers a vision of sexuality that goes beyond moralism and sexual exchange that characterizes much of our culture."[41]

This is the first time in the narrative of Scripture when a man and woman have been in a garden alone and the implication was not a sexual bonding. When we remember the closeness between Jesus and Mary for the few years preceding the empty tomb—it is utterly radical and *new* that they do not end up having sex when they meet alone in a garden—a place rich in meaning with sexual passion and union in the Bible. In their friendship narrative, *there is no resolution of the sexual tension*. Both liberals and conservatives want the tension to disappear into an eventual outcome—chaos or control. Conservatives feel the need to distance themselves from sex-free but deeply meaningful, passionate friendship because for one thing, it is a step away from the highly valued notion that sex is procreative—and they don't want to go down that slippery slope. On the other hand some liberals feel the need to distance themselves from sex-free but deeply meaningful friendship as an outcome because they see sexual repression as unhealthy and dangerous.

Suspicion comes in at this point—for those who see sex as the fullest expression of what it is to be human, when Jesus distances himself from

Mary. Post-Freud, to be human *requires* humans must have sex. For post-Freudians, in order for Jesus to be "fully man" he can't be a sexually repressed man. This popular view is eloquently expressed by *60 Minutes* commentator Andy Rooney, "The pledge of celibacy demanded of priests assumes that sexual desire can be suppressed by resolve. The fact is, sex isn't something a person can decide to have or promise not to have and then never have it."[42] Sexual repression on this side of Freud is dangerous for those who see sex at the center of what is means to be human: "Repressed persons are especially dangerous in positions of authority." Reading through a Freudian lens requires Jesus to have sex with Mary Magdalene or to marry her, precisely because a normal human being "without sexual expression, development, or fulfillment is a failed concept."[43]

But even feminist Janice Raymond, who champions lesbian intimacy, sees the need for passion to be dignified with full human freedom and will in friendship: "Passion is not deterministic, unless one holds to a very passive view of passion," she writes. She believes that if we view passion as overpowering the will, we can end up using it as an "excuse not to make choices." She suggests, "One can choose to be passionate friends instead of exercising passion in a sexual/genital way... This is not a 'watered-down' version of love. Because passion may not be expressed in a sexual/genital way does not make it immaterial or insignificant. Passionate friendship has its own depth and intensity and is characterized by strong feeling and, often, physical affection."[44]

Here in John 20, the story of Jesus and Mary Magdalene is full of intensity and passion. In the garden, Mary was weeping. These are not tears just for show or because she is emotionally weak. She has loved Jesus with a fierce love. And Jesus knew that. He has given his life for her. His death was not an abstraction. In her deep grief, Jesus welcomed her embrace. There was no need for a hurried, abrupt physical separation. This story reveals the intense display of love, passion, intensity, intimacy, and physical embrace. Jesus once again, is not fearful of his sexuality, of women, of intimacy, or of vulnerability. Can authentic intimacy between a male and female happen like this in the context of safety? That is, can a woman be safe from seduction by her close friend? The story suggests a sexual maturity of freedom, responsibility, vulnerability, and intimacy in friendship. Feminist and author bell hooks in her book, *Communion*, talks about deep, passionate, but sex-free friendships declaring them to "a threat to patriarchy and heterosexism because they fundamentally challenge the assumption that being sexual with someone is essential to all meaningful, lasting, intimate bonds."[45]

Jesus was ushering in sexual shalom in the new creation:

> Jesus said to them, "Those who belong to this age marry and are given in marriage; but those who are considered worthy of a place in that age and in the resurrection from the dead neither marry nor are given in marriage. Indeed they cannot die any more, because they are like angels and are children of God, being children of the resurrection" (Luke 22:34-36).

Without a doubt, this is a complex and committed male-female friendship full of redemptive intimacy. Many theologians and church fathers have taken a negative view of sexuality and used Jesus' rebuff of Mary to validate their oppression of women and distance from women in relationships—in marriage, friendship, and community. But with Jesus as her Lord and her intimate friend, Mary entered into something greater than mere friendship with a man. Unlike the first garden, there was a new dawn arising for man and woman.

We would do violence to this story if we forced it to say all that needs to be said about male-female relationships and sexuality. There are other stories in Scripture and tradition to affirm the beauty, goodness, and truth of marriage and sexual fidelity. This is not a story about the beauty, goodness, and truth of mutual sexual intimacy in marriage. It is a story about male-female friends not succumbing to irresistible passions and falling into sex or romantic love. However, it is all about communion: "One of the greatest challenges to us is that our sexuality become catholic." Catherine LaCugna also suggests sexuality is a "vital path to holiness, creativity, fecundity, friendship, inclusiveness, delight, and pleasure."[46]

This was not marital love. Nor was Mary Magdalene his mother or his biological sister. But this was the kind of friendship that says, "Where you go, I will go; and where you lodge, I will lodge; your people shall be my people, and your God my God" (Ruth 1:16). Her weeping was not the weeping of a sentimental, private, emotionally weak woman. This was not the casual, take-it or-leave-it, detached modern friendship between men and women. Proverbs18:24 informs us that "Some friends play at friendship, but a true friend sticks closer than one's nearest kin," and in this brave new (covenant) world dawning she happened to be *female*. Mary chose to put herself in this close, vulnerable position with Jesus. And, the resurrected Christ chooses to put himself in this close, vulnerable position with Mary alone in the garden. As C.S. Lewis has observed, that is what love does:

> To love at all is to be vulnerable. Love anything and your heart will certainly be wrung and possibly broken. If you want to make sure of keeping it intact, you must give your heart to no one, not even an animal. Wrap it carefully round with hobbies and little luxuries; avoid all entanglements; lock it up safe in the casket or coffin of your selfishness.[47]

That night Jesus called his disciples his friends. He assured them, "'Those who love me will keep my word, and my Father will love them, and we will come to them and make our home with them'" (John 14:23). Jesus reveals himself and therefore this distinctively fresh knowledge of God's story to his female friend and disciple, Mary. Here, knowledge of God is beyond our control or our mastery; yet in the friendship love between Jesus and Mary Magdalene, knowledge of God is immediate, personal, relational, direct, intentional, tangible, mysterious and glorious. The mystery of male-female friendship emerges as a relationship where God himself is revealed. In the presence of deep, sacred passion, Truth is revealed and known: "This is a knowledge that originates not in curiosity or control but in compassion, or love—a source celebrated not in our intellectual tradition but in our spiritual heritage."[48]

Mary began talking with a man she assumed to be the "gardener," but the veil was lifted from her eyes when Jesus spoke her name. In freedom and love the risen Lord revealed his resurrected self first to Mary. In the garden of the new creation, the female friend and devoted lover of Jesus' was the first one to "know." This knowledge had not been revealed to any of the male disciples first. At this moment on the eschatological clock, every one of the twelve male disciples still had a veil over his eyes. "Now the Lord is the Spirit, and where the Spirit of the Lord is, there is freedom. And all of us, with unveiled faces, seeing the glory of the Lord as through reflected in a mirror, are being transformed into the same image from one degree of glory to another; this comes from the Lord, the Spirit" (2 Corinthians 3: 17-18). Mary *knows* the risen Christ.

Jesus meeting with Mary has more to it than meets the eye—not as in the presence of sex, but in contextualizing sex—that is, *sexual union is not the only form of communion between man and woman in the new creation.* In the tension of the now and the not yet of the coming kingdom, the embrace between Jesus and Mary invites us into the drama of embodied love between man and woman to nonromantic nearness/ union in friendship: "Contrary to the conventions of his day, Jesus was not afraid to speak with or to touch women, even when he was alone with them and there was the greatest possibility for scandal and discrediting his ministry."[49]

This kind of sacred passion not only anticipates the new heavens and the new earth, but also the mystery of deep, embodied, spiritual friendships between men and women in this world. Our created bodies matter, not only in marital love, but also in friendship that goes forth into the Christian community and the world. "But go to my brothers and say to them, 'I am ascending to my Father and your Father, to my God and your God' (John 20:17).

CHAPTER 6

SACRED BODIES
AND FRIENDSHIP

"Through the body we draw near."
Lilian Calles Barger[1]

"Love dismantles boundaries."
Richard Beck[2]

"You gave me no kiss, but from the time
I came in she has not stopped kissing my feet."
Jesus Christ

It was my friend's turn to pray for me. I had just finished praying for her and she was beginning to pray for me. I had already been holding her hand while I had prayed for her. As she started to pray she moved her free hand underneath my hand and was now praying for me holding my hand with both of hers. I *felt* valued. I *felt* loved. I *felt* treasured. I *felt* her tender gentleness. I *felt* pleasure. I *felt* her energy for me. She was not just praying for me out of her head. She was not just touching me to make contact with me physically; her grasping my hands was corresponding to her heartfelt intercession for me. I heard the smile in her voice as she prayed for me, and I felt it in my hands.

Any spirituality of friendship between the sexes in the twenty-first century will not ignore our sacred bodies and their social importance in healing the deep male-female split in the church and the world. "At its deepest and truest level," writes Vincent Genovesi, "Christian living is an extension of the incarnation. This means that our lives are a continuation of Christ's embodiment of God's love for us."[3] Although he was a first-century Jew firmly situated in the social context of Palestine, Jesus' friendships with women were revolutionary. They deviated from the socially acceptable cultural and religious practices of his time which "forbade men and women from socializing casually in that world."[4] Jesus did not talk about friendship with women as something he could foresee as a social practice in the future for Palestinian community. Male-female friendship was not merely an idea or some inner desire with no social engagement for him. Jesus was not a spectator observing conventional protocol, expressing a theoretical openness to women.

While there were certain expectations of physical closeness in brother-sister relationships in the ancient world, "most cultures around the time of Christ fostered a climate inhospitable to authentic friendships between men and women."[5] All four Gospels provide amazing stories about Jesus' relationships with women set against the social and sexual boundaries of his culture. One striking feature in all four Gospels is the eye-opening range of physical nearness Jesus experienced with women who were not his siblings and who Scripture does not suggest were married. These are relationships we would call cross-sex friendships. "Friendship," writes Elizabeth Moltmann-Wendell, "then becomes a chance to understand incarnation anew and to experience it and allow it to be reflected in all of our lives."[6] The mystery of the incarnation is that God in Christ overcame the boundaries between heaven and earth, between spirit and matter, between flesh and spirit, *and* between men and women. Christ came into this world through a woman's body. And, these stories reveal his highly unusual (in light of his culture) physical nearness to various women during his ministry.

Nonromantic Physicality and the Way of Jesus

Jesus' practice of welcoming women, in addition to his male disciples, to follow him in addition to his male disciples from village to village was unheard of among Jewish rabbis. Kenneth Bailey comments that this is true even to this day in the Middle East: "Women can travel with a group of men but must spend their nights with relatives."[7] The traditional sex-segregated boundaries between men and women who were not kin were being reshaped by Jesus in this alternative path of eschatological oneness. Many communities required wide physical boundaries between men and women—especially if they were unrelated. Even if we include the positive portrayals of women and sexuality in the Old Testament, we don't find the nearness of male-female friendship as we do in the Gospels. Bailey quotes Ben Sirach instructed men who lived in the early second century B.C., "Do not sit down with women" (Sir 42:12).[8]

As we have seen, Jesus meeting alone in a garden with one of his female disciples, Mary Magdalene, before he saw his male disciples— is quite provocative in light of the deep ambivalence between men and women of his day. Jesus was in the center of a highly gender-defined culture. Jewish spirituality at this point in history was overwhelmingly male-focused, and situated in the broader ancient world; women were not thought capable of sustaining friendships. A plausible reading of Jesus' story in the Gospels suggests he encouraged risk and passion in the name of loving one another—that is, loving one's female neighbor. It is highly probable that Jesus shared a deep physical relationship with Mary Magdalene during the time she traveled with him and his disciples— not the physicality of romantic love but a deep physical connectedness of shared social space over the course of at least a few years.

The depth and breadth of the robust embodiment with which Jesus related to women is highly significant for cultures obsessed with sex. The Gospel stories offer a rich embodied distinction between sex and sexuality. These stories highlight Jesus' freedom and authority to live and practice an enfleshed, physical, concrete, nonromantic nearness with women in a culture that had no place to put such physical nearness and touch with one's female neighbor. According to Judith Plaskow, Rabbis taught, "He who has not married by age twenty spends all his days in the thought of sin."[9] Yet, we see something different in Jesus and his embodied love towards women. The same Jesus who warned men about the danger of lust "was not averse to having his body cared for in quite intimate ways at various times by various women."[10]

Jesus openly received extravagant physical affection from a woman in front of Simon the Pharisee, who thought her touch was inappropriate. Simon was squirming and offended; but Jesus was not embarrassed by her attention—he called it love. Jesus used the word *agape*. Simon was known for his religious purity, and it is clear that Simon believed there must be something impure underlying her touch:

> One of the Pharisees asked Jesus to eat with him, and he went into the Pharisee's house and took his place at the table. And a woman in the city, who was a sinner, having learned that he was eating in the Pharisee's house, brought an alabaster jar of ointment. She stood behind him at his feet, weeping, and began to bathe his feet with her tears and to dry them with her hair. Then she continued kissing his feet and anointing them with the ointment. Now when the Pharisee who had invited him saw it, he said to himself, "If this man were a prophet, he would have known who and what kind of woman this is who is touching him—that she is a sinner." Jesus spoke up and said to him, "Simon, I have something to say to you." "Teacher," he replied, "speak." "A certain creditor had two debtors; one owed five hundred denarii and the other fifty. When they could not pay, he cancelled the debts for both of them. Now which of them will love him more?" Simon answered, "I suppose the one for whom he cancelled the greater debt." And Jesus said to him, "You have judged rightly." Then turning towards the woman, he said to Simon, "Do you see this woman? I entered your house; you gave me no water for my feet, but she has bathed my feet with her tears and dried them with her hair. You gave me no kiss, but from the time I came in she has not stopped kissing my feet. You did not anoint my head with oil, but she has anointed my feet with ointment. Therefore, I tell you, her sins, which were many, have been forgiven; hence she has shown great love. But the one to whom little is forgiven, loves little." Then he said to her, "Your sins are forgiven." But those who were at the table with him began to say among themselves, "Who is this who even forgives sins?" And he said to the woman, "Your faith has saved you; go in peace" (Luke 7:36-49).

This is a story about forgiveness and love. Even more precisely, it is about a forgiven woman who expresses "great love" to Jesus. He didn't support narrow conformity to social boundaries out of consideration for public sensibilities. Scripture recognizes, "How beautiful upon the mountains are the feet of him who brings good news" (Isa. 52:7). Rodney Clapp observes, "attending to our feet strikes chords not only of humility and vulnerability but of poignant tenderness and beauty."[11] This story stokes our imagination. When Jesus validated her affection, he revealed to Simon that her embodied love was not evil or inferior, nor was her physical touch unclean, nor was she property to be dismissed. Jesus did not silence her physical language of passionate love towards him.

In the immediate context, the story was a response to the question the disciples of John the Baptist had raised with Jesus in Luke 7:19: Is Jesus the one Israel has been waiting for or are they waiting for another? Jesus told them the blind can now see, the crippled now walk, the lepers are healed, the deaf can hear, the dead are raised, and the poor have the gospel preached to them. Blessed is anyone who did not take offense at Jesus (Luke 7:19-23).

As Barbara Reid insightfully observes (and I am indebted to her for insight), the whole point of Luke 7:36-50, "hinges on Jesus' question to Simon in verse 44, "'Do you see this woman?'"[12] Simon, a Pharisee, continues to see this woman through the eyes of his community. That community rejected both John the Baptist and Jesus, "For John the Baptist has come eating no bread and drinking no wine and you say, 'He has a demon'; the Son of Man has come eating and drinking, and you say, 'Look, a glutton and a drunkard, a friend of tax-collectors and sinners!' Nevertheless, wisdom is vindicated by her children" (vv. 34-35). Simon did not see a forgiven woman who showed great love, but saw her as a sinner. Jesus saw her loving much because she had been forgiven much. If Simon could see this woman as Jesus sees her, then he would also see Jesus.

Simon, as a Pharisee, was not an isolated individual. He stood in unison with the collective social wisdom of his community when he did not see this woman as Jesus the prophet from God saw her. Simon was not a part of a secular community. His community knew the same sacred writings that Jesus knew. They revered the same sacred Scripture that Jesus revered. They revered Jehovah as the only one true God. So did Jesus. To the Greco-Roman communities of the day, Jesus and Simon were much alike than different. They were both loyal Jews. But the Pharisees thought Jesus was a pleasure-seeker out of sync with their standards of purity.

Within the span of a few verses, Luke links friendship, wisdom, women, full-bodied affection, and great love. The ascetic, pleasure-denying lifestyle of John the Baptist was equally criticized by the Pharisees. This should not be missed as our story introduces the impulse of physical pleasure, goodness, beauty, and love. In contrast to John the Baptist, Jesus was well aware of their *communal* disgust towards him. They saw him as one who *excessively* pursued pleasures and befriended those who were sinners, those who were impure. The text clearly indicates that Simon and his community considered Jesus to be seeking pleasure inappropriately. The fact that Luke tells us that Jesus was aware of this before the unnamed woman makes her appearance should not be over-looked.

Intensity or passionate bonding is associated in negative ways with women and friendship. In the ancient world, Nancy Tuana reminds us, the Greeks believed that "a woman left uncontrolled was one of the greatest dangers to mankind." She recalls that Aristotle believed that a woman was unable to control her passions through reason: "Thus, woman, left on her own, would be led astray by her passions, particularly her sexual passions, and in turn would cause great suffering to man."[13] Greeks believed "that the animal passions inherent in woman's nature could best be tamed by marriage. A proper union would domesticate woman by ensuring that her passions were properly controlled and directed toward the welfare of her family."[14] But there is no evidence the woman of Luke 7 was married.

While Simon labeled her a "sinner" Jesus never did. He did acknowledge her many sins, but unlike the woman caught in adultery in John 8, Jesus never told this woman "go and sin no more." Both Simon and Jesus (and indeed, even the woman in this story) would have been thoroughly acquainted with sacred wisdom from Proverbs 7:

> Then a woman comes towards him, decked out like a prostitute, wily of heart. She is loud and wayward; her feet do not stay at home; *now in the street, now in the squares, and at every corner she lies in wait.* She seizes him and *kisses him,* and with impudent face she says to him: 'I had to offer sacrifices, and today I have paid my vows; so now *I have come out to meet you,* to *seek you eagerly,* and *I have found you!* I have decked my couch with coverings, coloured spreads of Egyptian linen; I have *perfumed* my bed with myrrh, aloes, and cinnamon. Come, let us take our fill of love until morning; *let us delight ourselves with love.* For my husband is not at home; he has gone on a long journey. He took a bag of money with him; he will not come home until full moon.' With much seductive speech she persuades him; with her smooth talk she compels him. *Right away he follows her,* and goes like an ox to the slaughter, or bounds like a stag towards the trap (Proverbs 7:10-22, emphasis added).

The italicized words convey what would appear to be matching behaviors between the woman Simon saw and this prostitute. The woman was in the city and learned Jesus was at Simon's. She came in and begins to kiss his feet and anoint them with her own scented perfume. The parallels are worth considering for anyone who thinks Simon is obstinate or uptight. But wait. There's more for Simon to consider in the positive portrayal of female sexuality: "Let him kiss me with the kisses of his mouth! For your love is better than wine, your anointing oils are fragrant, your name is perfume poured out" (Song of Songs 1:2-3). She then wiped Jesus' feet with her hair. According to Middle Eastern custom, women were supposed to keep their head covered for their "hair exudes vibrations that arouse, mislead, and corrupt men."[15]

Simon, a representative of a male-centered, male-dominated culture, was seeking to control this woman's intensity and passionate physical expression. In any sexist, gendered culture, the conservative understanding of Jesus' openness to her whole embodied presence (her intentions, her impulse, her lips, her hair, her tears, the oil, her courage, her sense of when to stop the extravagant affection, and her sensual hunger) is immediately understood as an "out of control," with an "anything goes" attitude regarding the body and physical attention. Jesus' feet were mentioned seven times in this short passage. He was not embarrassed to receive her lingering attention and affection even when Simon thought it was disgusting. What is *not* happening—from either Luke's view or Jesus' view—is sexual disarray or chaos. Neither Jesus nor the woman has impulsively given himself or herself over to lust.

Anglican Brian Thorne wonders about this scene. He writes: "I suggest that men—especially thirty-year-old men—might fantasize what it would feel like to have their feet wept over by a prostitute and then rubbed and kissed by her continually (not just once or twice!)."[16] Andrew Greeley asks:

> Did he enjoy the emotional abandon of her sobs and tears, something definitely not part of the ordinary feet-washing ritual? I don't say how we can say he did not. If he were utterly unmoved by it, he would not be human. It was something she needed to do and he tolerated that. Presumably he did not want it as a daily occurrence. He surely knew when and how to indicate gently enough was enough, that her self-humiliation had gone far enough and it was time to stop. I wouldn't be surprised that she knew too. Erotic tension? Surely.[17]

Meanwhile, Lillian Calles Barger correctly observes it is "one of the most sensual scenes in the Gospel."[18]

In this encounter, Jesus didn't perpetuate the longstanding, deep-rooted sexism viewing women as sexual objects, mere property, or slaves to their passions. Although Jesus didn't return her expressions, he received her lavish outpouring of tenderness, warmth, closeness, and pleasure.

Is this story about more than forgiveness? Contemporary evangelicals tend to focus on this as strictly a conversion story in which the repentant female prostitute is in need of God's rich forgiveness, while the cold-hearted Pharisee, Simon, remains in the dark about his need to be forgiven. Is that all there is to this story? Is everything else in the drama between Jesus, Simon, and this woman, merely incidental details?

If we prematurely categorize this text as a story of forgiveness or conversion, we may completely miss out on the richness of holistic, authentic, embodied Christian sexuality and spirituality in friendship. Because conversion stories of dramatic and deep forgiveness are evangelical identity markers, it is tempting to isolate and highlight the "spiritual" transaction as the superior meaning. As someone who has been an evangelical for over thirty years, I've heard this story repeatedly emphasized in contexts of forgiveness and conversion. But I believe this story has some social import when it comes to sexuality, friendship, and male-female oneness. If we don't grapple with the embodied richness of this account of Jesus and the woman, do we not run the risk of reinforcing a social brand of evangelical Gnosticism?

To what extent does this story shape reconciliation between the sexes in the twenty-first century? We won't make much progress if we, as evangelicals, continue to spiritualize the unnamed woman and Jesus and emphasize the value of disembodied, abstract forgiveness. A number of contemporary women ponder embodiment and wisdom in Jesus' culture. Lilian Calles Barger observes, "In a society ruled by males, women were highly affected by both the rules regarding uncleanness and those governing marriage and divorce. Women with their monthly discharges and pregnancies were often in the position of being unclean. Nevertheless, Jesus spoke to and touched women instead of regarding their bodies as a problem."[19] Kristina LaCelle-Peterson writes, "if women are viewed only as objects of male sexual desire, of if they are blamed for male temptation, they are dehumanized and not treated with respect, let alone justice." She adds that Jesus "refused to treat women as sex objects or stigmatize them on the basis of sexual transgressions."[20]

Carrie Miles states, "Jesus opened the door not only to female discipleship but to the possibility of men and women interacting without reference to sex.... To Jesus, women were more than sources of impurity, temptresses, wombs, servants, hostesses, or whores."[21]

Why then, do we tend to exclude this story when we talk about holistic sexual maturity and *friendship* between the sexes? The stories of Joseph and Potiphar's wife as well as David and Bathsheba are front and center in every evangelical conversation about getting too close to the other sex. These stories should shape our social imagination about the dark side of nonromantic nearness. But why do these stories have the major social and spiritual significance in our churches? Why do they get the focus when evangelicals talk about male-female relationships outside of marriage? Is it morally good and beautiful for us to *welcome* physical intimacy from a person of the other gender when sex is not on the table? Perhaps Wyndy Corbin Reuschling has a point when she observes in her recent book on *Reviving Evangelical Ethics*, "I fear we have made the story of Jesus too familiar, too personalized, and too tame when it comes to moral deliberation. We have domesticated Jesus and made him into an action buddy."[22]

Jesus, Friendship, and the Virtue of Chastity

Against this background, Jesus, before Simon, is not a frigid prophet when it comes to sexuality. The verb "touching" in verse 39 is semantically related to the same verb in Apostle Paul's counsel to the Corinthians: "It is well for a man not to touch a woman" (1 Corinthians 7:1). F. Scott Spencer guesses Simon's inner thoughts: "It is well for a holy man not to allow himself to be touched—*in that way*—by a woman, a sinner-woman at that!"[23] Jesus calls us to a social righteousness that goes beyond the communal wisdom of the Pharisees and first-century Israel. *External* markers of perfume, kisses, and undone hair are not sure-fire indicators of sex on the mind or heart. Even passion is not always an indicator of lust or inappropriate sexual behavior: "To state the obvious, all demonstrably affectionate women are not harlots."[24] Here, Jesus is not going to fall into a cultural trap of insisting virtuous women are required to be stoic, detached, calculated, and masculinized in social sexuality. A robust, healthy chastity then, is not an abstract concept that fits into a one-size-fits-all, narrow definition of femininity, masculinity, and sexuality frozen in time.

Chastity has been used by men, by authorities, *and* by communities to marginalize women, their bodies, their friendships, and physical affection with men. Frank James, a contributor to the book, *Mixed Ministry* and former president of Reformed Theological Seminary, declares the focus of avoiding sexual temptation could be used as "an excuse to marginalize women.... I do worry a bit that behind the fear of temptation is a false view of female sexuality."[25]

Although the virtue of chastity itself has been reduced at times to avoidance strategies, this story is one of openness to the riches of embodied love greater than sexual gratification. This courageous woman's outpouring of love to Jesus and his ongoing willingness to receive it offer a deeper, more positive view of chastity than does a clear-cut resistance to all impulses of affection. Jesus did not allow Simon to stop the creative, mutual blending of chastity and physical tenderness. Paul Wadell laments that "many people associate chastity with sexual repression or even renunciation, as if chastity produces people who are uptight, prudish, and altogether uncomfortable with their sexuality."[26]

Jesus reframed the moral goodness and wisdom of pleasure and touch in friendship between men and women. Jesus engaged our social constructs of what is acceptable between men and women when he welcomed and validated the woman's impulse to kiss his feet *repeatedly* as her embodied expression of love and gratitude towards him. Today, perhaps Jesus would be in agreement with the postmodern philosopher Foucault (more than many conservatives would want to admit) when he said, "Society and the institutions which frame it have limited the possibility of relationships [to marriage] because a rich relational world would be very complex to manage."[27] The "rich relational world" of the Christian male-female spirituality present in this story was simultaneously unnerving to Simon and liberating to the unnamed woman.

Old Testament examples of kissing happen primarily among men in family situations. The few examples of kisses between men and women are romantic in particularly romantic or seductive contexts (Jacob kissing Rachel, the seductive kissing in Proverbs 7, and the kisses between lovers in the Song of Songs). The woman of Luke 7 *lingered* over Jesus' feet, kissing them, pouring expensive perfume on them, and wiping them with her unpinned hair. Brian Thorne believes her passion affected Jesus: "For him, the woman's behavior constituted an outpouring of great love. It is difficult to imagine a more powerful eruption of the sensual, the sexual and the physical world of social convention and legalistic morality, and as a physical, sexual and sensual being like us, Jesus must have been deeply affected by this extraordinary episode."[28]

This unnamed woman must have encountered Jesus prior to this night. His presence had awakened a desire in her that would not settle for the physical boundaries imposed by her religious culture and community. Perhaps she had seen Jesus talking to women. Or Jesus himself had talked with her before. We don't know. Jesus had awakened a desire of beauty and goodness in her to be near him, to be with him, to touch him, to physically connect with him—a way of friendship. She didn't desire casual sex. She didn't desire promiscuous sex. She didn't desire sex. Jesus didn't treat her touch as temptation or out-of-control lust. She did want to physically express to Jesus the tender feelings of her inner life. Jesus was as deeply acquainted with the stories of Joseph and Potiphar's wife, as well as with the stories of David and Bathsheba, as Simon would have been.

Jesus was modeling authentic and holistic embodied chastity. This virtue, according to John S. Grabowski, "enables human beings to use their sexual powers wisely and well. In so doing they contribute not only to their own flourishing, but to a well-ordered society that reflects God's plan for human sexuality."[29] This story clearly teaches us that chastity is not about clear-cut rules or about propagating sexual or gender stereotypes in male-female physical intimacy. Yes, it is always appropriate to flee from sexual temptation. It is appropriate to remember David and Bathsheba. Popular Christian thought conflates safe, risk-free living with a stodgy, once-and-for-all list of rules for chastity. Such thinking is a kind of fortress mentality. Thorne comments: "I often feel that it is in the arena of personal relationships that the Church's mission could be most powerful and yet it is so frequently at its most cowardly and most judgemental."[30]

What kind of male and female disciples do evangelical communities produce when they teach the Bible as a book of rules concerning our embodied sexual selves? What passes for contemporary chastity in many churches reflects old, stereotypical fears about women, sexuality, friendship, and our bodies. For example, the evangelical megachurch, Saddleback Community Church, calls for their staff to follow sex-segregated rules pertaining to men and women's bodies. Four of them read like Billy Graham's rules from the 1950s:

- Thou shalt not go to lunch alone with the opposite sex.
- Thou shalt not have the opposite sex pick you up or drive you places when it is just the two of you.
- Thou shalt not kiss any attender of the opposite sex or show affection that could be questioned.
- Thou shalt not visit the opposite sex alone at home.[31]

It should be duly noted that these don't apply to those who are single. And why not? Apparently, at least one assumption has to be that singles of both sexes are free to mingle with one another without any presumption of sexual scandal. In addition, these rules would undermine an adult single's abilities to date unless accompanied by another adult. Many Christians no longer believe it is inappropriate for paired men and women to be alone together in numerous social contexts. Many Christians welcome and practice nonerotic behaviors when they are alone.

What was once clearly considered to be inappropriate by conservative Christians is now accepted as appropriate behavior. Holding hands, kissing, back massages, foot massages, any kind of physical contact that doesn't come near what some call the "bikini line" (that is, parts of the body covered by a bikini) are considered to be appropriate expressions of love and commitment without irresistibility leading a dating couple into something inappropriate. All physical behaviors wisely avoiding the bikini line are considered by licensed counselors as helping adults remain "soul virgins."[32] If you are dating and physical touching stays above the "bikini line" presumably, you have a decent shot at maintaining emotional, spiritual, and physical purity of bodies and souls while you *meet alone.* The talk among Christians of boundaries surrounding the bikini line assumes that a man and woman will spend time alone with each other (since very few Christian men and women are blatantly tempted to cross the bikini line in public!). Christians assume men and women, in private, can be morally accountable to each other without the sexual police around. Many Christians have sorted out the *appearance* of possible "dangerous" behaviors (kissing, petting, hand holding, cuddling, back and foot massages, and so on) between two unescorted adults from clearly erotic behaviors (involving genitals and breasts) which ramp up the desire for immediate gratification and consummation.

But Saddleback's boundaries for married adults seem to convey the depths of a sexual fundamentalism. Although there is no question there are good intentions towards wisdom behind these boundaries, they produce rule-driven, sex-segregated communities. As Wyndy Corbin Reuschling reminds us, "Christian virtues have something to do with Jesus Christ." She writes, he "is our frame of reference for explicating the quality, shape, and *telos* of virtues we should nurture in order to call them *Christian*."[33] We have already seen some of the Gospel stories where Jesus talked with women alone when no one else was around. Jesus' reception of the woman's repeated kisses clearly called into question Simon's own convictions (and his community's) about appropriate behavior.

The story of Christ inspires us to think much deeper about a robust chastity, moral goodness, beauty, and "great love." This woman and Jesus provoke us to think about possibilities deeper than black-and-white boundaries, sexual police in faith communities, or cookie-cutter discipleship.

Although Elizabeth Elliot was not intending cross-sex behavior in the following statement, her wisdom should be heeded as we consider transmarital friendships and boundaries: "Let us not be Pharisees in our certainty of what God could or could not permit."[34]

In Jesus, we see that a gospel-centered chastity, which involves a creative physical openness towards the other gender is not to be casually dismissed. This is not just an *idea* about something that should happen in the future. Embodied openness to the other sex in friendship and (and not merely disembodied "spiritual" practice) is at the heart of intentionally overcoming ambivalence, indifference, fear, and hostility. We see respect for the goodness of nonromantic affection and touch between men and women as a path of chastity for friendship, not something to be feared. Before Simon's eyes was a Jewish male who embraced his sexuality "without diminishing and distorting his sexuality into self-centered carnal satisfaction."[35]

The reign of Jesus draws men and women to the profound beauty and depth of gospel-centered chastity in friendship. Within rule-driven, sex-segregated communities, the physical and emotional estrangement between men and women falls far short of moral formation and ever-deepening reconciliation. The Gospel story anticipates a resounding "yes" to respectful, chaste, embodied, maturing love between men and women. "Faith awakens trust in the still unrealized possibilities in human beings—in oneself and in other people. So faith means crossing the frontiers of the reality which is existent now, and has been determined by the past, and seeking the potentialities for life which have not yet come into being."[36] While Christians are now beginning to warm up to the idea that sex is not dirty, that sexual desire and pleasure are good and beautiful in marriage, the next significant step toward a chaste authentic sexuality is to embrace the goodness and beauty of desire for embodied connection with our most cherished cross-sex friends.

The Shape of Embodied Chastity in Friendships
Dan Allender uses the metaphor of chaos to describe a world fallen into

sin—which obviously includes sexual disarray and instinctual sexual desires gone astray. In his book, *Intimate Allies*, he suggests that "marriage partners either call order and beauty out of chaos or intensify chaos." He believes husband and wife are to shape the other towards beauty and goodness out of chaos.[37] It struck me that this is, in a nutshell, what the virtue of chastity is all about in forming cross-sex spiritual friendships. Jesus was nurturing order and beauty as he received this woman's physical attention. Unlike Simon, who saw her as still stuck in sexual chaos, Jesus saw her beauty and welcomed her chaste but passionate affection.

The shape of embodied chastity is an honest openness to the beauty of the other. In *marriage*, this honest openness is what opens the door for ever-deepening, passionate, tender, sweet, maturing sexual love with a flesh and blood person. As we choose to be open and vulnerable with our bodies, we learn to let our guard down, we begin to bare our bodies, our emotions, our fears, and our desires. As we surrender our entire embodied selves we discover the utter depths of one flesh. We learn to give ourselves over to our spouses and to receive their embodied selves in a beautiful, deep rhythm of ever-widening giving and receiving. If we are not open to the risk of giving ourselves and receiving, we may never dive into the deep waters of the profound mystery of mutual delight and oneness.

The virtue of chastity invites us to ongoing, loyal giving and receiving as we open ourselves to the beauty of the other: "While man and woman are bound in intimate union in innumerable ways, each is, at the heart of their relationship, utterly free. They *choose* to love one another. Each must also *choose* to speak boldly to the other if either begins to see the spirit of mutuality being betrayed."[38] The wedding night does not magically create a full-blown, mature openness no matter how heart-stopping the sex. As Philip Rolnick observes, "Interpersonal communion would be meaningless if it were automatic."[39]

This openness of giving our embodied self, and receiving our spouse's embodied self, needs to be cultivated. The media saturates us with images of what is attractive, beautiful, and "hot." Kristina LaCelle-

Peterson laments, "All too often churches buy into cultural ideas about thinness, beauty, and femininity as well."[40] This is not openness to chaste embodiment but enslavement to cultural pseudo-beauty.

To be open to meaningful touch in transmarital friendship in private and public is to reclaim our bodies for wider, broader, and deeper meanings of physical presence in God's world. "Reclaiming" means our bodies encompass much more than meanings of physical intimacy in casual sexual relationships or the self-absorbed romantic myth. These categories tend to depersonalize and desexualize men and women in male-female relationships. It's easy to identify the casual relationship as sexual chaos, as impersonal and sexually inauthentic. But Christians in rule-driven communities where there is an appearance of order have a tendency not to see the chaos inherent in conformity to abstract rules. Their orderliness makes a persuasive case to protect the sexual beauty and integrity within marriages. This is what is attractive for so many who embrace the sex-segregated boundaries within churches like Saddleback. This safe, risk-free chastity "works" for many in our contemporary churches.

Yet, there is another form of sexual chaos and we see it in our story if we listen closely. If we enforce all embodied interactions between men and women with clear-cut rules of distance, then we will be left with this huge dichotomy between the personal and the impersonal in embodied male-female relationships. In other words, if Simon gets his way, we don't get to see the personal uniqueness of this woman's "great love" for Jesus. At least part of what makes this story so powerful and liberating is Jesus' beautiful, personal, unique meaning and description of her physical affection. This was a moment between Jesus and the sacred body of this woman. No one would say that Jesus was cavalier about sex. This story is not about escaping temptation. It's about this woman's beautiful outpouring of personal attention to Jesus and his body. "Ecstatic exaltation can be present in all forms of human love. In personal love, ecstasy comes from being fully in the presence of the other person rather than from being in love."[41]

In my understanding, as I have read the reactions of female theologians to this passage, one of the most striking elements in this story is personal embodied engagement that takes place between Jesus and the woman. She pressed forward with great courage, with much to lose, expressing her "great love" to Jesus, the God-man. Picture the scene. Kiss after kiss, tears flowing, oil being applied, and her hair released from her veil to wipe Jesus' feet. As Alvin John Schmidt observes, "The four sexist characteristics of woman being 'evil,' 'inferior,' 'unclean,' and 'unequal' need to be recalled if one is to gain a better understanding of the reasons for women having to be veiled."[42]

After the first "ahem," Simon sees Jesus is not getting it and lacks social prudence and discretion; therefore, he can't possibly be a leader— a prophet of God. When did Jesus finally respond to Simon's inner thoughts? After the first ahem? Second? Third? Jesus' welcoming of these sensual acts, not just one of them—but all of them, reveals a dance in which he relaxes the social boundaries between a *man* and a woman—at a *woman's initiative*—that doesn't have anything to do with sex. At some point in this drama, Jesus' "yes" to her ongoing impulses draws out more of her embodied self and her social choices. John Grabowski explains the difference between a chastity stuck in the law versus a more holistic, personal, and social chastity:

> When law becomes the dominant paradigm for the moral life, chastity takes on a different meaning. Chastity becomes that virtue that safeguards one from the violations of the law concerning the matter of sex whether inwardly or in external conduct. Rather than a dynamic principle enabling one to use one's sexual powers intelligently in pursuit of human flourishing and happiness, chastity is seen as a form of conditioning that elicits adherence to extrinsic rules that restrain human freedom.[43]

If it is appropriate to use stories like David and Bathsheba to ground our understanding in the forming of chaste relationships between the sexes, then this story in all of its chaste richness must also be included in our understanding of a robust sexuality and chastity so that we may

avoid depersonalizing and desexualizing by categorizing individuals
into groups and communities. As more Christians return to the deep
and rich value of community there is going to be a danger of impersonal
chastity. Friendship is an important moral relationship with the ability to:

> nurture for another a self they never were allowed to believe they
> had.... There is no better way to affirm the value and worth of
> another person, no surer sign of our affirmation of their goodness,
> than to be willing to receive the offer of their attention as a gift.
> Sometimes, perhaps surprisingly, it is our willingness to be available
> to their love that leads to some of the richest and most powerful
> moral experiences of our lives.[44]

A holistic, embodied chastity does not rigidly conform to impersonal
categories, principles, or even groups. At the heart of this story is an
embodied expression of a personal relationship between Jesus and the
woman. The story shapes interpersonal embodied depth and chastity
between men and women who are not lovers. The practice of chastity
reflects the glory, beauty, goodness, and truth of triune love and the
inexhaustible richness of our created, sexed, sacred bodies. Therefore
chastity cannot be anti-body, anti-physical, anti-sensual, or anti-sexual.
Vincent Genovesi suggests, "Too often people neither appreciate nor
capitalize upon the unique richness of human sexuality."[45] Any twenty-first
century vision of chastity must acknowledge this fact. This richness of
divine beauty in human sexuality is surely accessible in romance and
marriage but also in nonromantic male-female relationships: "Personal
relationships are relationships of freedom and equality in which *persons*
choose how they relate to each other. The essence of personal relationships
is responding to others freely, uninhibited by societal prescriptions."[46]
If we don't allow stories of redemptive embodiment to shape our
communities, ethics, and sexuality, we run the danger of domesticating
and impersonalizing chastity.

This story, as the breadth and depth of the Christian story, reminds us
of the eschatological chastity that men and women are moving towards.
It informs us that virtue participates in a holistic freedom towards the

other sex in meaningful response to personal goodness, beauty, and truth instead of conformity to abstract communal rules and social categories. Truth is Personal and Relational.

This bigger picture of chastity then, says no to all forms of sexual chaos including impersonal categories imposed by communities or cultures. Where conservatives tend to fall short is that they only see chaos in sex expressed without commitment and marital vows. They don't see chaos in impersonal conformity to sub-incarnational embodiment. The incarnation is not only concrete and sensual, it is eternal Beauty, Goodness, and Truth breaking forth into the old ways of the world and community: "The very dynamism of human life is established because we are in relation with God who is infinite truth, goodness, and beauty.... The very purpose of humanity is thus caught up in the quest for *more than*.... Friendship must go forward in pursuit of more truth, beauty, and goodness so that ever greater gifts of the self can be given and received."[47]

Chastity, then, becomes the relational skill of choosing freedom to dance with personal beauty, goodness and truth in embodied relationships. Chastity summons us to see the wonder, amazement, and utter beauty of eschatological touch between Jesus and others in the Gospels. Notice Jesus' touch in healing Simon's mother-in-law: "Now Simon's mother-in-law was in bed with a fever, and they told him about her at once. He came and took her by the hand and lifted her up. Then the fever left her, and she began to serve them" (Mark 1:30-31). Jesus reached out to a woman and took her by the *hand*. This is a profoundly personal moment. People commonly died from fevers before modern medicine. Jesus could have spoken a mere word. But he engaged her skin, her embodied self. No matter what this woman experienced in her body from this point forward—including sex with her husband, this embodied nonsexual touch full of eschatological beauty, goodness, and truth, no doubt, remained with her as a significant moment for the rest of her life. She would never forget the meaning of this simple, personal touch.

Neither should we.

For those who are married, at least one of the reasons why many women have not experienced orgasms or find it difficult could be the impersonal and unchaste approach to sexual pleasure by husbands who see sex primarily as proving their manhood and expressing their own passion. The impersonal pervades our marriages when women are "naturally" perceived as the half of the human race with a lower sex drive. Modern society categorizes men and women into impersonal categories. Touching the other, in this sense, even when the man experiences orgasm, is highly impersonal. This doesn't mean every time a husband and wife have sex they have to achieve mutual orgasms. But the spirit of mutually invited touching the sacred body of the other is the practice of chastity in marriage.

But in the evangelical subculture, singles are encouraged and socialized to view members of the other sex in impersonal categories of either romantic potential or married. This, too, is another subtle but powerful form of sexual chaos instead of practicing the virtue of chastity. This virtue calls us to personal, meaningful, intentional, embodied engagement with opposite sex friends—and not merely according to impersonal categories. A bigger dimension to sexual or nonsexual touch in Christian sexuality is its eschatological meaning of personal beauty, goodness, and truth in the moment and the larger personal context. Impersonal categories like romantic potential or marriage discourages the beauty of chaste freedom to touch in *personal* relationship. Inauthentic chastity emanating from sizing people up and placing them in impersonal categories is just as much of an expression of sexual chaos as out-of-control lust. These false boundaries are inauthentic precisely because they are impersonal.

For some singles then, there is a tendency to stay away from meaningful intimate touch with the other sex in the present moment unless it has romantic potential. Just like sex in marriage, touch in friendship could be characterized by impersonal, inauthentic expressions towards another. The gift of touch in authentic Christian chastity is not expressed in two different kinds of chastity: premarital and postmarital. The virtue of chastity before marriage prepares and shapes us for chastity within marriage: "Spouses are, ideally, chaste nonvirgins."[48] While a chaste individual recognizes the limits of touch with her cross-sex friend, she simultaneously doesn't reduce her friend into impersonal categories. The practice of embodied, chaste touch for us all, including singles, requires a "delicate balance between caution and risk, between inhibition and daring vulnerability."[49] Ronald Rolheiser suggests that "the impression is given that sexual union is happiness and no happiness is possible outside of that. That is a superficial and dangerous algebra." He adds later, "We need to express affection, we need to touch each other physically and we need to affirm each other more explicitly ... to stroke each other physically and emotionally into wholeness."[50]

Chastity in both friendship and marriage empowers us to give ourselves to the other "in a way specific to their own vocations." John Grabowski suggests it "makes possible the integration of one's sexuality into the commitments that structure the person's life. In so doing, chastity makes it possible for persons to discover the communion for which they were created."[51] Both within marriage and friendship a disembodied sexuality (i.e. sexual chaos) then, "further distances us from the responsibility of dealing with the demands of another person's presence, denying both intimacy and body. The principle of chastity mitigates against this."[52]

The husband and wife share a unique, unrestricted, fullness in their sexual intimacy that they don't share with anyone else. They cultivate a sexual bond that is off-limits to everyone. As they renew and refresh their vows in sexual love, they model triune love: beauty, oneness, fidelity, loyalty, permanence. However, this *openness* to the beauty of giving and receiving of our embodied selves extends beyond the sexual intimacy in marriage. As Lilian Calles Barger notes, there is a "deep communal significance beyond the couple." She rightly points out the extraordinary breadth of authentic openness in chastity: "As we image God in our sexuality, we experience our profound human capacity to enter into a variety of life-giving and life-receiving relationships, but this deep, life-affirming connection extends to all human beings and is not expressed only in the act of sex."[53]

Spiritual friendship between the sexes in the twenty-first century can be a powerful, chaste embodied witness to the sexual chaos in our sex-obsessed culture on the one hand and the over-romanticized impersonal culture on the other. In nonromantic contexts, male and female friends who are open to the beauty and goodness of touch embody intimate chaste, meaningful touch in private and in public— this is sexual formation of calling beauty out of the sexual chaos of casual sexual boundaries and impersonal categories. Even though popular evangelical wisdom suggests otherwise, embodied formation of one's sexuality doesn't merely occur in marital sex or romantic love: "Friendship is itself a specific form of self-giving between persons, and in this way is formative of a person's sexuality."[54]

So singles who practice chaste touch with their single or married cross-sex friends may experience more *personal* depth in friendship than some Christian married couples who have sex. Sex, as we saw in chapter two, is not the major indicator of personal, holistic communion: "Intimacy is primarily about attachment, not sex."[55] Sex does contribute to communion and can open the door to profound union, but sex in marriage is not a magic pill for inter*personal* wholeness and communion. But in friendship, a single individual is not shut out from the deep communion of embodied beauty, goodness, and truth with the other gender even when there is no sex involved.

While marriage is certainly a relationship in which profound intimacy may happen, in friendship singles are able to experience profound depths of beauty, goodness, and truth if they open themselves to the risk of embodied personal intimacy with the other sex. Many leaders in the evangelical subculture, however, discourage singles from this risk in intimacy and thereby set up singles to relate in terms of impersonal categories, inevitably creating a social dichotomy between singles and married. In the process of writing this book, I have been encouraged to hear a growing number of singles who desire meaningful, embodied beauty, goodness and truth in friendship with the other sex instead of holding themselves back while they are waiting for romance and marriage. To open themselves to the desire and risk of beauty in the other, they enter the profound dance and adventure of embodied, intimate friendship.

Arthur Roberts, professor-at-large at George Fox University, in his excellent thought-provoking book, *Messengers of God: The Sensuous Side of Spirituality* suggests we need role models for physical intimacy in friendships in our churches to overcome the stereotypes. The emphasis upon sexual touch in either casual sexual relationships or romantic relationships, Roberts says, has impoverished our lives greatly:

- By minimizing friendship as an experience basic to mere social civility, maximizing adversarial processes.
- By narrowing perceptions of sexuality to genital intercourse, fostering predatory tactile behavior.
- By maintaining a stereotypical focus upon genital sex roles, adding confusion to nongenital friendships so that … men and women cannot be considered close friends without being suspected of having a romantic affair.[56]

This is sexual chaos and disorder in friendship and community. The romantic myth popularizing Freud's theories has romanticized and sexualized all affectionate, meaningful, tender, and gentle physical affection—*physical* and *personal* intimacy between men and women. Barger notes, "With no nonerotic way to receive necessary human touch, we set up for indiscriminate sexual activity."[57]

More and more Christians today are seeing the truth that James Olthuis wrote in 1975: "The myth that all close contact necessarily leads to physical intercourse is just that—a myth." And then he too, notices how this myth has imprisoned Christians, "We must *free* ourselves from its deadening influence. Friendship is a God-given way to be intimate which does not involve sexual intercourse" (italics added).[58] Love in friendship is directed towards the embodied other in personal relationship— not impersonal categories. Friendship is one of God's formative paths to heal the split between the spiritual (important, internal, higher meaning) and the sensual (unimportant, external, and superficial) between men and women.

Teenagers clearly see this disembodied sexual chaos. Kenda Creasy Dean, associate professor of youth, church, and culture at Princeton University says, "The church's *de facto* decision to let popular culture define passion as sexual intimacy has disastrous theological consequences. On the one hand, separating body and spirit tends to reduce to 'parts and plumbing'—the usual content of church-sponsored sexual retreats— as the human desire for otherness becomes associated with biology rather than identity in God."[59] She insightfully adds, "When sexuality is primarily a matter of biological function, affirming sexuality (which Christian doctrine requires) means celebrating body parts, while at the same time telling teenagers not to use them. Teenagers are quick to see the inconsistency."[60] They only see two alternatives for physical affection between adults in the community: scant physical contact because of impersonal categories or romantic expressiveness. The evangelical church by and large has basically accommodated the romantic myth and Freud by relegating all close, social markers of physical touch/ presence to be sexual—either promiscuous or romantic. In the evangelical community we primarily give our bodies to the other sex in public when romance is happening. We are embarrassed, afraid, or ashamed to express the beauty and tenderness of a nonsexual immediacy of our sexed bodies between friends in public. Our teenagers witness this disembodied sexuality in practice in many communities.

Chastity calls us to give ourselves in love to the sacred body of our spouse and then, out of a spirit of mutual embodied connection, the embodied immediacy of our friends. While this immediacy honors the integrity of limited touch in friendships, the eschatological dimension of embodied chastity guides us to an ordered fullness of goodness, beauty, and truth in these personal relationships—in marriage and friendship. Chastity is the freedom "to respond to and nurture the beauty and potential that I see in another human being."[61] Freedom in friendship is not the pursuit of unrestricted touch, like the freedom in marriage, but the freedom to create and redeem freshness of embodied beauty, goodness, and truth in the other sex in personal relationship. "Intimacy," writes Arthur Roberts, "occurs significantly among friends through manifold sensations of touch.... Touch gives intimacy to friendship."[62] In the following quote from Ruth Haley Barton, I am going to replace her original word, "love," with chastity:

> *Chastity* is not sentimental slop that goes wherever emotion and physical urges take us. It is not the stoic and sometimes sterile way we often speak about 'loving our neighbors as ourselves' while keeping our selves at a safe distance. Rather, it is the kind of *chastity* that engages others on spiritual, emotional and physical levels. It is a *chastity* that opens us to the beauty in each other and compels us to reach out in meaningful and appropriate ways. *Chastity* calls us to hold each other in God's presence regularly and to take responsibility for ourselves so that we never intentionally do anything to hurt or defraud another person or their significant relationships.[63]

SEXUAL SHALOM
AND FRIENDSHIP

"There will be great harmony between angels and virgins,
inseparable friendship, inestimable love,
untold sanctity in holy embraces and kisses.
Between youths and virgins, men and women,
unmarried and married."
Groscelin of St. Berlin[1]

"It is therefore easy to see why Authority frowns on friendship.
Every real Friendship is a sort of secession, even a rebellion."
C.S. Lewis[2]

"True subversion requires patience. You slowly get cells of people
who are believing in what you are doing, participating in it."
Eugene Peterson[3]

I have made the outlandish suggestion that there is more to oneness in male-female relationships and sexuality than just sex or marriage. The journey towards sexual shalom requires navigating across the complex terrain of unity and diversity in the new creation. I opened this book with my former pastor's claim that the Bible and tradition were very clear. But with a deeper look at God's story and history, the picture that emerges is quite different from what he sees as clear. Sexual redemption for men and women as created to be sexually embodied has a much broader scope than just the formation of romantic couples. I believe there are Christians who hunger for deeper discernment in sexuality and male-female friendship. In the context of the kingdom, male-female friendships are a foretaste of the sexual shalom we are all moving toward. This is not the "order" of social distance and physical frigidity in female-male relationality. But it is also not the disorder of violence, irresistible urges, adversarial touch, or social inequality. "Friendship," writes Liz Carmichael, "is the overcoming of all its varied opposites: fear, strangeness, and alienation, enmity and hostility, and indifference."[4]

In their book *Placing Friendship in Context*, authors Rebecca Adams and Graham Allen write, "Relationships have a broader basis than the dyad alone; they develop and endure within a wider complex of interacting influences which help to give each relationship its shape and structure."[5] Christ came not to just reduce the old disorder of lust, violence, and oppression between men and women, but to usher us into a new world of embodied communion with each other. As Laura Smit observes, "From now on, our orientation must be toward the future, the promise of the New Jerusalem. The changes that Jesus introduced are far reaching, and one area that was changed forever was marriage." She adds, "Jesus is not only the fullness of God in human form but also the one who shows us the fullness of humanity. Yet he never marries."[6]

The path towards sexual shalom is a calling to be real corresponding to our identity as men and women living together in Christ. As Kevin Vanhoozer observes, "disciples are nothing less than witnesses to eschatological reality, to the new creation inaugurated by the risen Christ."[7] Following Miroslav Volf's suggestion, it is simply inadequate to attempt to set up ideals of femininity and masculinity as we seek to form life-giving male-female friendships: "It is precisely the one triune God in whose image all human beings are created who holds the promise of peace between men and women with irreducible but changing identities."[8]

If Volf is right, then our imagination for friendship must not settle for gender stereotypes in ways of practice, identity, or community. Christian male-female friendship centered in the communal love of the Father, the Son, and the Holy Spirit calls us to go beyond current social differences between female friendships and male friendships. Forming nonromantic relationships means we step into a dance of co-creativity and freedom between the sexes in friendship, community, and culture. For some, this will appear to be a call not to shalom but to chaos and uncertainty. For others this will appear to be a romanticized view of friendship unattainable in faith communities. Yet, there are too many "already and not yet" stories for us to ignore, dismiss, or rationalize as too idealistic. There will be those who attempt to marginalize the power of these stories by claiming they are "exceptional." Yet in the gospel "the glorious impossible"[9] has already happened in Christ. When Jesus came into this world he did the unthinkable. With God, all things are possible, and these stories witness to the fearful, the cynic, the doubter and the curious. Chaste, passionate, enduring male-female friendships bear witness to the powerful, redemptive love which should be normative, not exceptional, for his people.

In that light, there are several Christian practices to form, foster, and nurture cross-sex friendships. This is not intended to be an exhaustive list. It's not uncommon to see these same practices recommended in books on same-sex friendships, but rarely are they suggested for nonromantic, close male-female relationships.

Hospitality

Friendship is simply not possible without hospitality. To practice hospitality towards the other sex (i.e. the "stranger") is to participate in a revolutionary kind of love and friendship. It could be that hospitality is where it all begins. Cultural niceness, courtesy, and friendliness are often as deep as it gets between men and women in Christian community. As David Matzko McCarthy notes, "Friendliness is the American way of making contact without getting close."[10] Polite friendships never require us to intentionally open ourselves to the other sex—and they never shape our communities or change the world.

Although men and women gather together to worship in Christian communities every week, estrangement lurks just behind the pleasant demeanor we wear. Hospitality flies in the face of the underlying divisions between the sexes in contemporary culture. *Men are from Mars and Women are from Venus* according to popular wisdom. We don't communicate well with each other because we are from two different planets metaphorically speaking.

Further, because of the sexual brokenness among Christians, the suggestion of opening ourselves to our opposite sex brother or sister in Christ is actually unnerving to some. We are urged to erect boundaries of self-protection, spouse-protection, marriage-protection, etc. Brian Walsh and Steven Bouma-Prediger make an interesting observation about boundaries in general. "Boundaries used to erect fortresses of self-protection," they write, "can never be refuges of hospitality."[11] Dan Allender makes an even more startling claim, because it comes in the immediate context of healing from sexual abuse. He makes it clear that there is a legitimate place for boundaries in relationships. But he draws a radical difference between secular and Christian boundaries. "The objective must be," he writes, "to bless the other person rather than to make sure we are not abused again. We are to draw a boundary in order to better love the one to whom we are relating." He adds, "*To love is to be more committed to the other than we are to the relationship, to be more concerned about his walk with God than the comfort or benefits of his walk with us.*"[12]

The practice of hospitality in cross-sex friendship requires risk; it is not an invitation to express cultural niceness. We don't have to deny that we hurt and wound each other in our relationships. As Paul Wadell observes, "we can be failures at love." But that is not the final word on who we are or on embodied love between friends. He adds that we are called to "a revolutionary love, not a safe and cautious one."[13] This kind of opening ourselves to the other is not an invitation to stay forever in unhealthy or abusive relationships. There are degrees of risks, degrees of safety, and degrees of danger. All of us are imperfect lovers and therefore, imperfect friends. Healthy trust and robust intimacy does not happen overnight.

Unromanticized hospitality in Christ summons us into the redemptive ambiguity, paradox, mystery, and dance of male-female relationships in our faith communities and in the world. On the cross, Jesus says to his mother and the disciple whom he loved, "'Woman, here is your son.'

Then he said to the disciple, 'Here is your mother.' And from that hour the disciple took her into his home" (John 19:26-27). Tradition has it that this disciple is the Apostle John. How old is John at this point? Just three years earlier, he was fishing. Most believe he lived another 60-70 years after this. How old is Mary? Tradition has her giving birth to Jesus at a very young age. By some accounts she may be only in her mid-forties. It's quite possible we have a man in his thirties taking a woman in her forties into his home (about the current ages of Demi Moore and Ashton Kutcher—as I write this they are one of Hollywood's most celebrated couples). Here is a vivid example of non-romantic male-female nearness and hospitality in the kingdom.

Our homes and the depths of our hearts may open to our cross-sex friends. My single friend lived with us for six weeks when she moved into this area while she was waiting to move into her apartment. Are we able as adults to open our homes to our friends with trust in each other? Mature brothers and sisters in the Lord who are committed to chaste, loving friendships should be blessed with the freedom and trust to open their homes to each other without suspicion or chaperone. Ambiguity. Mystery. What about the possibilities of singles joining married couples to live together as households of faith? Singles and married couples may form their own micro-community in hospitality and not live as separate, autonomous units that so dominate our culture. What David Matzko McCarthy observes about friends in general certainly applies to singles, married couples, and hospitality: "Good friends join together in a common vision that outsiders some-times consider elitist, exclusive, a threat, or just difficult to understand." He envisions friends who "start to live, struggle, and move forward side by side with the same way of envisioning the future ... they seek a goal that is beyond each and attainable only together."[14]

Confession/Forgiveness

I share a mutually deep confessional friendship with my wife Sheila, and also with several women friends (single and married). We confess personal sins—against each other, and committed against others. We mutually confess our weaknesses, failures, mistakes. We also share our hearts, many of our inner secrets, desires, fears, hopes, and pains.

Confessional friendship, both inside marriage and in addition to, involves different risks. The danger here is that men are generally socialized to experience emotional closeness through sex. The experience of emotional intensity draws such men into the desires for sex if they are not able to separate vulnerability and bonding from sex. Is confessional intimacy with our cross-sex friend inherently dangerous, or could it rather be a relational practice of truth, beauty, and goodness? Contrary to the fears and opinions of some, lust is not a "hard-wired" inevitability when deep emotion is present. To acknowledge we are not inherently dangerous to one another does not remove the risk of sex but it does require us to be responsible for our desires and sexual maturity. A more nuanced and balanced view comes to light in the medieval spiritual friendships between priests and women. These relationships were not intense short-term friendships. They were long-lasting and intense with no sex. In these relationships, confidences were shared, confessions were deep, and communion developed.

Confessional bonding is not all about our weaknesses or sins. It is about the longing and yearning for more. In my close friendships with single women, I allow their passionate desires to be "visible" to a good man. In their hearing I bring their desire for romance, for marriage before the Lord: "The actual details of intimate needs and relational realities become the stuff of prayer. Desires are shaped into adoration and difficulties are formed into petitions."[15]

The practice of confession has broader risks than just sex. Eugene Peterson suggests that seeking intimacy at any level, with God or others, "is not a venture that gets the support of many people. It is inefficient."[16] As we express vulnerability, there is no guarantee that the other is going to meet and connect with us. "The dance of mutuality is always drenched in vulnerability and risk because it is a non-coerced meeting of two free subjects in the wild spaces of love."[17] Our friend may not receive what we intended and vice versa. Or even if they understood what we intended, they still may not be in a position to receive our good intentions or confession. They may not be able to see goodness and beauty in our actions in our vulnerability. Honest mistakes may happen where we might not see the beauty of the friend's intention or they ours.

In the Christian story forgiveness is a significant practice for male-female friendship. Yet, as Paul Wadell laments, "We are often more skilled at nursing hurts than offering forgiveness, more skilled at plotting revenge than risking reconciliation."[18] John Swinton comments, "Friendship is the place where forgiveness begins." Forgiveness is the practice that opens the door to the wide ranging and diverse possibilities of confessional friendships in male-female oneness. Yet, forgiveness is also an issue for women who have "forgiven" and "forgiven" to stay in unhealthy, abusive relationships with men in marriage, and friendship. Appeals to forgiveness fall on deaf ears with some when other Christian practices are not evident or functioning in the relationship. However, we must observe that a practice of forgiveness "does not let hurts, betrayals, divisions, and disappointments have the final word."[19] It still remains true in the Jesus story that forgiveness does not at all slight the offenses but nevertheless enables flawed lovers to pick up the pieces and rebuild relationship:

> We seldom think of friends when we hear Jesus' admonition to love those who hurt us, but friendships can help us learn what it means to love those we find it hardest to love, even our worst enemies. First of all, aren't there times when even our best friends can seem more like enemies than friends? In the history of every friendship there are moments when the relationship is characterized by animosity more than benevolence, bitterness more than peace. Friends can hurt one another deeply.[20]

Male-female relationships are fraught with potential pitfalls, misunderstandings, and disconnects—in marriage and outside of marriage. Yet there remains the high reward of goodness, beauty, and truth to pursue in confessional friendships. The research of Daniel Stern and others indicate for example, that *all* babies—not just girls—*yearn* for relational connection and intimacy. On the one hand, what is crucial in any of kind intimacy is a self-giving, a "self-sacrifice" in order to walk into the profound depths of oneness, of shared vulnerability. On the other hand, there is a delicate balance between owning our individuality in Christ and self-denial so that turning the other cheek means we end up with an unhealthy relationship. These don't have to be relational dead-ends. The beauty of forgiveness and reconciliation may enter into any relationship currently snarled in fusion.

As men and women form confessional intimate friendships with each other in marriage and transmarital relationships, we have to confess our fears, risks, desires, longings, frustrations, and hopes. Some spouses, for example, who wrestle with insecurities will want to keep their mates on a "short leash" when it comes to cross-sex friendships beyond the marriage. There are simply no formulas, no rules, no boundaries that can *guarantee* marital safety and fidelity. The ideas in this book are dangerous. Friendship is dangerous. Yet, with all the rules, boundaries, and simplistic formulas in place in certain faith communities, one still finds adultery. This is true not only in their marriages but in their theology and spirituality—control is all about seeking to do away with uncertainty or chaos. They have to have it all figured out and in control before they enter something.

Confessional intimacy however, is not a static or frozen concept. It is dynamic. It moves. It changes. It flourishes or dies. Confessional intimacy deepens our trust, our "we-ness," our "with-ness." It is not about moving into rigid postures, nor is it about railroading the other. No spouse should turn the other cheek to the point of becoming a doormat for the sake of any friendship beyond marriage. In a posture of vulnerability our own hearts are stretched to give to the unique other and to receive from them in ways of authentic freedom we could never have imagined. So, as we saw in chapter four, healthy marriages do not exist as romantic couples clubs, or ends in and of themselves, but as avenues to care for and love each other in our faith communities.

Delight

It may appear to some as hopelessly naïve or dangerously unrealistic to suggest in a book advocating transmarital intimacy in male-female relationships that we as Christians need to grow in our practice of delighting in the other. Yet the Christian practice of delight has for various reasons fallen on hard times—particularly delight in marriages and in cross-sex friendships. In much of popular culture, delight is genitalized and over-romanticized. In some sense, this book is an invitation to sexual formation and the practice of delight. In another sense, it is beyond the scope of this book to adequately do justice to such a neglected and misunderstood practice. Much more is needed to explore the depth of delight in twenty-first century male-female relationships.

Delight in our cross-sex friend is not lust. Some in the Christian community confuse the two, conflating lust with delight and therefore fearing the awakening of delight in male-female friendships—and reinforcing romantic stereotypes and behaviors.

One way of approaching beauty in sexuality is to reduce it all down to avoid lust, responses to beauty, and meaningful engagement with women: lust and sin management within marriage and beyond. We find similar avoidance strategies among medieval men: "The mere sight, touch, or sound of a woman was thought to be potent enough to provoke concupiscent thoughts or, worse, instant fornication."[21] This is another glaring area where our sexual theology is too small, too narrow, and too fear-centered. The avoidance strategy regarding beauty leaves us with an impoverished, neuterized, and lust-driven view of sexuality. There are several reasons for rethinking delight in our opposite sex friends.

First, Christian delight begins not with physical attractiveness or sex, but rather with the triune God's radiant and glorious beauty. The intimacy and delight within the triune community are breathtaking, and we will forever and ever be 'lost in love and wonder,' in response. Following Gregory of Nyssa, David Bentley Hart suggests that divine beauty "inflames desires...stretching out toward an even greater embrace of divine glory."[22] Before modern rationalism overpowered language in the church, sexual imagery and language concerning God were common among medieval saints. Christine Gudorf reminds us that many of the Christian mystics "used very sexual language—even orgasmic language—to describe the relationship between the mystic soul and God."[23]

Second, Hart suggests, "it is delight that constitutes creation, and so only delight can comprehend it, see it aright, understand its grammar. Only in loving creation's beauty—only in seeing that creation is truly beauty—does one apprehend what creation is."[24] Then he adds an important insight into delight that distinguishes it from destructive lust: "In learning to see the world as beauty, one learns the measure of love that receives all things not to hold onto, not 'for me,' but as beautiful in their own splendor."[25]

Third, in light of the previous points, there is a God-given, distinctive, unique, and glorious beauty in every man and woman. This is not the plastic, artificial, or pseudo-beauty of popular culture, but rather a unique God-created and God-redeemed beauty in each of us. This is the genuine, authentic ground for delight in the other within marriage and in friendship; it is centered in God's own delight in us. Norman Wirzba suggests, "To take delight is finally to relish the goodness and beauty of God's work and to see in each other the trace of God." He adds, "The practice of delight presupposes a radical departure from all utilitarian calculation of benefits to self and a devotion to the building up and strengthening of others."[26] Authentic Christian practice of delight, then, recognizes the wild, God-given beauty of the other in their respective vocations of marriage and friendship.

Fourth, the practice of delight involves cultivating an attraction for the good and beautiful in the other sex. The dangers of lust and objectification of the other are real and genuine. In our quest for deepening sexual authenticity in marriages and beyond, divine beauty calls us to see others for who they uniquely are with unexplored depth, "rather than for what we want them to be or in terms of how 'useful' or pleasing they are to us."[27] Delight is not blind lust which is driven by a desire to possess, manipulate, and use for selfish pleasure. Delight is the passionate desire to intentionally take time and make space "to *discover* her as other and *discern* what respecting and responding to her 'otherness' requires."[28] In this sense, delight honors the singular uniqueness of the other seeing them as God sees them.

Understood in this light, the practice of authentic delight itself shapes and marks out the boundaries for enjoying the supreme beauty in every male-female relationship, including both marriage and friendship. True delight in our spouses is the strongest boundary between all other relationships beyond our marital vows. In the bigger picture, true delight in our spouses creates a bond even deeper than the bond of sex. We all know of cases of married individuals who have had good sex with their spouses while they were sleeping with someone else. When we discover and discern the true delight of the other in a shared identity of "we" in marriage, the beauty of this "we" takes priority over all other individuals and deep friendships. True delight honors the distinctive primacy of the unique dignity and beauty of our spouses.

True delight though, unlike the self-absorbed, inward-focused delight of the romantic myth, can also be discovered and discerned in our friends beyond marriage—including our cross-sex friends. Attraction and delight in friendship as a moral, chaste love is documented in many nonromantic Christian friendships. A wonderful thing happens as authentic beauty awakens in marriage. It is possible to delight in the goodness and beauty of our cross-sex friends. An important step in sexual maturity is our discovery and discernment of the beauty in our friend, entering into their mysterious beauty while embracing the fidelity of delight towards both our spouse and our friend.

In other words, a deepening and maturing delight towards our spouse is not threatened by the inclusive delight of another's beauty in friendship —it is rather the basis for it. The goodness and beauty of a micro-community begins to form and take shape. The moral courage to pursue goodness, righteousness, and beauty for transmarital friendship flows out of the mutual intimacy of the marriage itself. In the heart of such marital intimacy, we are not threatened as our spouses begin to open themselves up to the richness of another cross-sex friend's unexplored beauty and glory.

For singles likewise, God's beauty invites them into the dance of love in which they open themselves up to discover and discern the beauty of the other sex. In the evangelical community singles have been conditioned to believe that true delight with the opposite sex is only found in marriage and put their skills of practicing delight on hold. In many communities authentic delight towards the opposite sex is not allowed outside of romance; it is dangerous. Yet, if the practice of true delight does not use others for our own sinful gratification, then a whole new world of possibilities opens up for the single individual to give and receive delight in cross-sex friendship. Ruth Haley Barton suggests, "Friendliness, intimacy and even appropriate sexual energy are normal elements of deepening relationships and should not be confused with openness to a sexual encounter."[29]

This side of Freud and the romantic myth, cultural notions of delight means for singles that if they are not married, they are missing out on authentic, deep, meaningful, satisfying delight. Popular messages in the evangelical community parrot the same notions about delight, sex, and romance. An evangelical single woman expresses it well:

> Many single women are conditioned to believe that their lives are insignificant because they lack a man's romantic affection...Single women are encouraged to put themselves out there 'in faith.' So, they make perceptive attempts to connect with men on a romantic level, rendering themselves vulnerable to those who might dismiss them on the immutable properties like personality and appearance. Women also hear that singleness is a punishment for those who have not attained a certain level of spirituality. Single women often live with a sense of inferiority, wondering what defective aspect of their lives has made them privy to the horrors of partnerlessness. Most damaging is the notion that singleness is something

unpleasant to be endured, like swallowing a bad-tasting pill or walking through a foul-smelling tunnel.[30]

In the romantic myth narrative, romantic delight trumps all other expressions and forms of delight hands down. All other relational delights are reframed as dramatically inferior, inadequate, or insufficient. Again, delight in romantic love is declared to be the *only* relationship that is the closest thing to heaven on earth—which is why so many singles experience depression and inferiority. Is this in fact, what Christian sexuality and spirituality has to say about delight, or is it a post-Freudian message obsessed with starry-eyed romantic idealism? In a hyper-romanticized culture to suggest deep, enriching, nonromantic delight is possible comes across as being antisexual, antisensual, or Gnostic. We have to ask, is there is an honest hunger for truth for the breadth and depth of delight in the Christian story? Is there a wider and deeper range of delight for Christian men and women? Is it always wise to avoid deep delight in close friendships with the opposite sex if one is married? Are all singles confined to biblically imposed prison cells of superficial and shallow delight with the opposite sex? Is our hunger for truth greater than our embrace of cherished ideas about romance and delight? Are we listening to the wide range of delight in narratives of Christian spirituality?

As much as the romantic myth is deeply embedded in our popular culture and in the evangelical community, there is no such thing at this point as a singular, monolithic cultural view. There is no such thing as "the Culture."[31] Our neighbors are beginning to discover more passionate depth is available in nonromantic male-female relationships in the twenty-first century than the stereotypical romantic messages of the twentieth allowed for. Lisa Gee in her book *Friends: Why Men and Women are from the Same Planet* believes that deep male-female friendships "are as beautiful, valuable and deserving of celebration as *any romantic attachment*" (italics inserted).[32] William Rawlins, another proponent of enduring, edifying, satisfying cross-sex friendships, believes men and women "may be known, befriended and/or loved for reasons and attributes that transcend sexual relations."[33]

Luci Taylor talks about her close male friend: "Yes, he's a man and I'm a woman. We're both heterosexual. We're very good friends. And we're not doing it—never have, and unless the proverbial pigs start to fly, never will." She suggests something that twenty-first century Christians on this side of Freud and the romantic myth need to process afresh. She suggests the possibility that an immature possessiveness in marriage impedes a more mature way of approaching transmarital male-female friendship: "This unhealthy possessiveness is just about forgivable when you're in school or in your 20's, when you can still get away with the excuse of chronic insecurity, but supposedly mature adults should know better. A partner should never be treated or regarded as a possession."[34] Psychologist and author David Benner writing from a Christian perspective observes, "Our husbands and wives are not our possessions." He suggests that while the biblical metaphor connotes a deep shared intimacy, "it should never be understood to suggest that two people become one person."[35]

Could it be that evangelicals have so overemphasized romantic love and delight, idealizing it as the only wise and pure form of oneness and soul friendship, that single men and women miss out on deep delight in their Christian experience and relationships with the opposite sex? Goodness, beauty, and truth in Christian spirituality is rarely if ever, about pat, black-and-white answers and rigid postures. Dan Allender suggests, "Rigidity is a refusal to reframe; it is a kind of thinking that limits the range of options and implications."[36]

Could it be that in our legitimate desire to affirm the goodness, beauty, and truth of sexual delight within marriage and honor that intimacy, we find ourselves closer to the narrow, reductionistic, immaturity of the romantic myth? The themes of nonromantic male-female nearness we looked at in chapter four and the powerful stories of mutual delight in male-female friendship in church history suggest a richness and depth in nonromantic delight. The evangelical community has perpetuated stereotypical ideas of romantic delight and sex that have resulted in many evangelical singles starved for delight, affection, and companionship with the other sex. And for many the wait has been long—and getting longer. Chaste cross-sex friendship fills the void of delight.

Elaine Storkey quotes Ecclesiastes 6:14-17, "Faithful friends are a sturdy shelter, whoever has found one has found a treasure. Faithful friends are beyond price. No amount can balance their worth. Faithful friends are the elixir of life, and those who fear the Lord will find them. Whoever fears the Lord will make true friends, for as people are themselves, so are their friends also." She then observes, "The images are powerful: *priceless, protective, intoxicating, immeasurable, faithful.* That such extravagant language should be poured out in praise of a relationship so neglected in modern Western society suggests that we have some rethinking to do. For the Bible makes it clear that intimacy between friends is one of the richest ways of knowing *shalom*—that deep sense of God's peace and well-being."[37]

While the Bible declares, without apology or embarrassment, the goodness and beauty of sexual delight between a man and woman in a covenantal relationship (Song of Songs), it also highlights without apology and embarrassment the profound, life-giving, enduring, nonromantic deep delight in friendship. This goes against the grain of the romantic myth. In the world of that myth, deep delight only knows one song and dance. But the Bible identifies deep delight and shalom in friendship. This counters strong messages of romance as the be all and end all as we looked at in chapter two. And, as David Naugle observes, *"immersion in contemporary culture, especially of the popular kind, radically influences our perceptions of happiness.*[38]

An authentic, catholic, Christian sexual maturity which follows the way of Christ includes a robust imagination and freedom in delight that is much deeper and broader than both the constraints of the modern romantic myth or the fears of sexual brokenness. The way of Christ is not to call singles into the principal's office or place a 911 call to the spiritual police in our faith communities if they open themselves up to delight in friendship with a married individual. Opening the path to deep delight in friendship is not the same as acquiescing to the notion that sexual delight or energy is irresistible. Many Christians simply accept that delight towards the other sex means we place ourselves in a position where delight or pleasure overpowers our reason and will.

This lack of control is at the heart of avoidance strategies and simplistic, black-and-white rules between men and women in nonromantic relationships. Christine Gudorf is one of many who remind us that this "argument that sexual pleasure is irresistible simply is not true. Humans frequently resist sexual pleasure, men as well as women." She lists several common examples. For example, she correctly notes, "Longtime lovers scoff at the idea that sexual pleasure can't be resisted, because resisting immediate sexual pleasure is essential to being a good lover." If we insist on maintaining that sexual pleasure is uncontrollable it leads to many problems. This notion is especially problematic for women who are victims of violent rape and sexual harassment. She notes how this lack of control assumption, "is often an attempt by men, and even by sympathetic women, to cut some slack, to allow them to vent some of the pent-up pressure in a sexual outlet. For too many males the concept of uncontrollable male sexual desire is the only alternative to sex as a kind of performance, a test of expertise, without spontaneity or intimacy."[39]

Opening ourselves up to deeper levels of delight in friendship with the opposite sex does open the door to authenticity, intimacy, and mystery, and that does not come without risks. Surrendering the false security of control in order to enter into deeper mutual delight in friendship is not surrendering our entire selves to the slippery slopes of carnal pleasure or inappropriate vulnerability. Negative stories are often related to substantiate the fear of those possibilities. But, if we refuse to acknowledge the sacred delight of triune love, the sacred delight Christ had in women, and the maturing and holy delight between believers in countless nonromantic stories in church history, we end up genitalizing and romanticizing all delight between men and women in marriage, friendship, and community. The practice of authentic delight in friendship is an active, mutual, surrender of our bodies, and our hearts to the nuanced dance of pleasure in goodness, beauty, and surprise. It leads us to experience the ongoing depths of delight in friendship. In naming our failures, our flaws, and our fears we paradoxically open ourselves up to discover the paths of true and authentic delight.

Redemptive delight doesn't run away from the unpleasantness or the dark side of pleasure. If we accept narrow definitions of delight between men and women in faith communities, we are not listening to the richness the transforming gospel offers male-female relationships. We are selectively staying within our own comfort zone. Redemptive delight in cross-sex friendship is a profound mystery to be respected, celebrated, and practiced. We need a deeper and broader authority in our sexual theology to embrace this deep delight in our evangelical communities rather than one-size-fits-all, tried-and-true avoidance strategies. More and more evangelicals are beginning to warm up to the idea that sex is not a dirty word. *Authentic delight in cross-sex friendship is not dirty, either.*

The wonderful reality of heart-shaping delight is that it presupposes friendship love forms and shapes us no matter where we are or who we are in our Christian journey. In God's story delight towards the opposite sex in marriage, friendship and community is a subversive practice in the sense that we actively recognize beauty in the other as God-given. As we cultivate delight in the other we see God's delight in them, and we behold the reality of God's beauty in them. Norman Wirzba reminds us that delight is in the details. "We can't really take delight from a distance or in a condition of apathy or ignorance ... If we are to see others with this depth, we must be prepared to get close to them and learn to see them for what they are."[40] Delight is subversive because it sees God's beauty in others according to God's delight in them and not according to cultural ideas or images of beauty.

In marriage, then, a growing and maturing delight as saw in chapter four is a holistic delight in our spouses—including seasons of surrendering to the intoxication of sexual love and desire as we see in the Song of

Songs. The lovers see and behold each other's beauty and desire the other in the fullness of sexual delight and love. The abundance of the other's God-given beauty opens the door for deep shalom. In seeing our spouse through God's beauty and delight, we practice a subversive delight that is counter to the market-driven sexuality in the media. The messages we are constantly bombarded with define attraction and beauty as thin, slender, busty and young. M. Gigi Durham observes, "Sexiness, desirability and ultimately *worth* is tied firmly in our mainstream media to the achievement of the slender, taut, bosomy, and ultimately Caucasian Barbie body."[41] This is the dark side of cultural beauty. In this way, Lisa Graham McMinn reminds us, "beauty is a beast that pursues and terrorizes them [women], convincing them they are not lovable or worthy of love if they are not 'beautiful.'"[42]

In friendship, delight is both a passive and an active response to the triune God's transcendent glory and goodness encountered within one another. Delight is a way of knowing and being that shapes our embodied selves toward the fullness of the coming sexual shalom in the new heavens and earth. God's story for both male and female encompasses much more than sex or marriage. It's important to let this notion—that delight is the way of the heart—sink in, especially when it comes to the new creation. Delight is a complex, layered, multi-dimensional virtue. It does not look the same in all relationships or for all people. It can't. The way of the individual's heart has unique grooves, channels, boundaries, wounds, memories, joys, and fears. Yes, we can talk about general patterns and socializing patterns. However, delight birthed, nurtured, and sustained in mutual, God-honoring sexual formation is the way of the heart, and all of our stories, all of our hearts are unique.

Delight is a wild, mutual dance. Delight receives. Delight gives. Delight may deepen. It has profound depths in both marriage and friendship. Genuine delight received from a cross-sex friend stretches our heart's capacity for the other in dynamic, maturing sexual shalom. Opening ourselves to the intellectual, emotional, spiritual, or physical delight offered to us from our cross-gender friend opens our embodied

Chapter 7: Sexual Shalom and Friendship

selves to the journey toward embodied communion in friendship. Although there are physical limitations in friendship outside of marriage, there are also profound depths of unexplored mystery and knowledge in friendship yet to be tasted and experienced no matter the age of a friendship. To think otherwise is to arbitrarily close ourselves off to the unending quest for beauty, goodness, and truth in friendship.

There will be some in our evangelical communities who cannot wholeheartedly and freely embrace this practice of delight. Not everyone wants to take the risk of surfing the ocean waves. Some may be afraid, while others are genuinely unequipped for its challenges. Others may not want to take the risk of downhill skiing. Still others will not want to take the risk of riding in a hot-air balloon. For many social and psychological reasons, others will not open themselves and their bodies to dancing. Others who have extraordinary artistic gifts are afraid to open their senses to their creative energy because their faith community has taught them to fear imaginative expression. In certain faith communities, authority squelches creativity and risk in spirituality. Just because some are not ready or are stuck in fear doesn't mean others should not experience risk, growth, and adventure, and drinking the depths of embodied delight with their cross-sex friends.

Are Christian communities nurturing authentic sexual maturity when it comes to deep delight in marriages and friendships? Or are they nurturing twenty-first century men and women to remain immature in their male-female relationships? The danger of using authority to shame cross-sex friends, by denying the goodness, beauty, and truth possible between them, is the age old problem of pharisaical righteousness and legalistic control in Christian spirituality. It fails to identify, recognize, and nurture maturing delight in friendship, and is in danger of maintaining the conventional status quo and missing God's inbreaking beauty, goodness, and truth. It runs the danger of replicating the old instead of saying yes to the new creation. And it runs the danger of being unable to discern and encourage individual maturity.

Paul Wadell reminds us, "The difference between being infantile in the moral life and being an adult is that the morally mature person does what he or she genuinely discerns to be right and good, not just what persons in authority claim they ought to do." He adds, "Instead of being like a child who unquestionably submits to the authority of others, a person of mature conscience freely commits herself to what she honestly discerns to be true and good."[43] Are we nurturing a wide range of diversity in freedom, maturity and delight in our communities? Delighting in the other is a dynamic dance, a journey of spiritual and sexual maturity. As individuals, we all start from different places. Friends may form unhealthy patterns of relating without sex ever entering in the picture, but this does not mean they will remain that way forever. Some friends unintentionally cross boundaries. Nurturing the practice of confessing and forgiving each other emerges as a maturing path towards a healthy, mutual delight in friendship and community.

Play

Authentic delight leads quite naturally into opening ourselves up to play. Play, according to Stuart Brown, is apparently purposeless (i.e. it is done for its own sake). It is voluntary and also involves, inherent attraction, freedom from time, diminished consciousness of self, improvisational potential, and the continuation of desire.[44] Within this context, play draws different kinds of responses from us: surprise, pleasure or good feeling, and intentionality. We gradually surrender our sense of awkwardness as we connect. Brown suggests, "Really making emotional contact with people, inviting an emotional closeness either in a casual situation or long-term relationship, requires that we open ourselves up to them. It requires that we not put up defensive walls and that we accept others for who they are. Then we can invite others to engage in play."[45]

The practice of play is, according to Kenda Creasy Dean, a transcendent practice that leads "to boundary-breaking experiences as they invite us to reach beyond our comfort zones into the new and mysterious world of the 'other.'"[46] A strong, healthy Christian view of play between friends will mean intentionally "ceasing" from obligations in order to just hang out, relax and enjoy. That's part of what it means to play. If we see play as a practice of redemptive goodness and beauty oriented towards eschatological joy and oneness, it becomes a mutual, cooperative, practice of rest and relaxation between male and female friends—i.e. the nurturing of the Sabbath rhythm in paired male-female friendship or one's circle of friends. Like the miracles Jesus did on the Sabbath, this redemptive goodness compels us to rethink previously held ideas about what is creatively possible as far as social rest and imagination are concerned. When Jesus practiced redemptive goodness, he disrupted social norms and challenged ideas about what it was appropriate to desire and do on the Sabbath.

In the overwhelming majority of marriages, spouses pursue friendships beyond marriage. Same sex friends do many things together in their dyadic friendship that they don't do as a threesome or foursome. They may develop Sabbath habits and rhythms of play in the practice of their friendship. There are a number of wide-ranging play activities adult same-sex friends do together without their spouses: concerts, day-long hiking, meals at anytime of the day or night, fishing, running, hunting, shopping, theatre, and the list goes on. If both friends are married, there is no need to have their spouses come along. There is a simple enjoyment and relaxation of being in the presence of one's friend and either doing things together or simply hanging out with each other for the sake of paired friendship play.

When I have pursued practices of paired play with a same sex friend and then later on casually shared our experience with another friend in conversation, I've never had someone ask me, "Why didn't you include Sheila?" Or, "Was Sheila not around when you went fishing with your buddy?" Or, "Did Sheila not want to go with you to the game?" Husbands and wives in our contemporary culture usually don't give it a second thought when their spouse goes to play golf or tennis, etc. with their close friend.

However, these are exactly the kinds of questions I have encountered when I have had "play" days with my cross-sex friends. Sheila has bought me tickets as a Christmas gift to enjoy a concert with one of my close single friends, as has my son. A married friend and I spent the day enjoying each other and creation as we went to Orcas Island in Washington. I have gone to Cubs games on separate occasions with both of these women. As of this writing, I have enjoyed many days of canoeing, hiking, shopping, or just exploring with my single friend.

Sometimes, I get asked why I have the "need" to do this apart from Sheila? Is that supposed to be some form of amateur psychologizing? Why don't I get asked that question when I do things with my same-sex friends? This question has more to do with assumptions about cultural romantic norms than Christian maturity, freedom, spirituality and sexuality. When a married individual and a single individual start to play the openness of the practice draws out the legalism, rules, and lists of do's and don'ts deeply embedded in the minds of some.

Play between paired cross-sex friends is another practice which subverts the immature possessiveness of the idealized couple in the romantic myth where the only socially approved nonromantic male-female "pairing" is family (i.e. brother-sister, father-daughter, mother-son, etc.). The myth allows no room for play in cross-sex friendships unless of course, an appropriate romantic trajectory is possible. Then adult cross-sex "friends" can play.

Does authentic sexuality in the Christian story *require* husbands and wives to limit the practice of play to their same sex friends and their biological families? Why would that necessarily constitute fidelity? Again, restricting the practice of play between adult cross-sex friends seems to constrict marital love, freedom, and responsibility as well as friendship love, freedom, and responsibility. Lewis Smedes suggests, "Between adultery avoided and fidelity never achieved, lies a spectrum of fascinating relationships between men and women."[47] If we imagine a virtuous spouse to be overly cautious, uptight, and unlikely to take chances we run the danger of quenching the Spirit of liberty and life in marriage and in friendship.

Do we want Christian spirituality, sexuality, marriage, friendship, community, and our witness to the world to be enslaved to surface appearances? Is there a deeper hunger for truth, for righteousness, for freedom, for goodness, for beauty in Christian sexuality and spirituality beyond conformity to crippled paradigms of relating? Deep within the social changes of the twenty-first century are questions about how Christian communities engage authentic friendship, marriage, play, and ordered social forms of love. Isn't play, a holistic vision of play, more than anything else the *holy* alternative to legalism and utilitarianism? "Play," Mark Buchanan writes, "is also subversive. It hints at a world beyond us."[48] Again, the trouble is when we take all the images and realities of male-female oneness in the Scripture and reduce them into a single concept—marriage. Kevin Vanhoozer argues that evangelicals must avoid this kind of reductionism in theology.[49] Evangelicals must also avoid it in the practice of male-female friendship, too.

I set aside days for just hanging out with my female friends when we do things like same-sex friends might do. As Kenda Dean remarks, "play contributes to a serious business of constructing the self."[50] Play and the *much more* of Christian spirituality and sexuality are deeply intertwined in the new creation.

Relational Prayer

Another practice men and women can enter into together is relational prayer. Many virtues are formed and shaped in prayer between friends. Gareth Icenogle observes, that "prayer and sexuality are deeply interconnected."[51] Paul Wadell may startle some when he suggests, "The deeper our life in God, the deeper our intimacy with one another. This is why, to put it bluntly, for Christians, intimacy begins not with sex but with prayer."[52]

There have been scores of books written in recent decades on the discipline of private prayer. While private prayer corresponds to Western values of individualism, you will find very few books on communal prayer or mutual prayer intimacy in spiritual friendship. It's almost impossible to find books on prayer and male-female friendship. Yet, relational prayer, it stands to reason, is a social form of intimacy where man and woman can hunger after God, hunger after goodness, beauty, and truth in their personal lives, in friendship, in communities, and beyond. Relational prayer in paired friendship is a communal discipline, distinct from isolated, private prayer.

My closest women friends and I practice relational prayer—we are prayer partners. We have rich times of prayer and each friendship has its own expression of what the prayer intimacy looks like and how often. One does form the capacity of deep listening in this intimacy. Just like sex, there is no shortcut to intimacy in becoming skilled in this discipline. In the *The Blue Parakeet*, Scot McKnight suggests we add "listening" to the Apostle Paul's description of love in 1 Corinthians 13:4-7. It would look like this:

Listening love is patient;

Listening love is kind;

Listening love is not envious or boastful or arrogant or rude.

It does not insist in its own way;

It is not irritable or resentful;

It does not rejoice in wrongdoing, but rejoices in the truth.

It bears all things,

believes all things,

hopes all things,

endures all things.[53]

As I write this, I have a treasured friendship with a married woman who is a mother and seminary student and currently we pray once a week. We have had a rich prayer life for several years now. We have prayed through many scenarios in our lives.

One of my single friends and I have prayed together for many years now, I feel like we are just beginners wading into the ocean of divine beauty, love, and authority. Currently, we meet once a week to spend unhurried time in mutual prayer. To listen to each other is an intentional practice of hearing and entering into the other's desires, fears, hopes, longings, and dreams; anything else on our hearts that we choose to share, we pray for each other. We share ourselves; we hold hands while we pray, as we seek God's presence together as man and woman in friendship. We also seek to pray daily for each other by phone. We are in this daily practice counting on each other as friends to help us each cope emotionally, spiritually, and physically with the experiences and tasks we encounter in this dark world, acknowledging we don't have the power to do this on our own.[54] There is a flourishing interdependency between a man and woman in spiritual friendship.

Here again, male-female relationship is shaped by trinitarian intimacy. David Cunningham in an essay on "Participation as a Trinitarian Virtue," suggests:

> If I ask you to 'take part in' my life, I am asking for a very significant degree of emotional, physical, and spiritual intimacy. This is the idea of participation that I am attempting to call forth: not working alongside others in a common activity, but of dwelling in and being dwelt by, one another.... If we express a desire to 'be in communion with' others, this implies more than simply spending time with them, more than just a sharing of mutual interests or good feelings. Rather, it implies allowing others to shape our lives in a profound and fundamental way. Under such circumstances, the lines of identity between 'me' and 'you' are blurred.[55]

When friends begin to open themselves to this deep love, two can become one, even if there is no sex between them. The greatest depth of oneness exists in the triune God, we see this in the paired relationship between Jesus and the Father: "In the beginning was the Word, and the Word was with God, and the Word was God" (John 1:1). Eternal *with*-ness. With-ness full of moral and spiritual excellence. This cannot be an unhealthy with-ness. This is the mystery of love—difference with profound face-to-face connection: "Like the Trinity, we are called to understand who we are not as isolated individuals who have to make contracts to protect ourselves, but as persons with faces turned towards God and each other."[56] Here, John highlights the *paired* eternal *with-ness* of Jesus and God: distinct but forever *with* each other. Apparently, in the eternal dance of with-ness in the Trinity, we can at least acknowledge Jean Baker Miller's belief, "You can never have too much of a good connection."[57] Women's friendships (whether they be same-sex or cross-sex) come under criticism periodically as immature and intense. Yet, there is an aching, a need, a hunger for deep *with-ness* beyond marriage and within it that reflects the eternal depth of *with-ness* between Jesus and the Father. We should be careful not to be critical of a nonsexual hunger for with-ness in male-female friendship. Passionate, cross-sex friendship stories witness the compelling mystery and complexity of male and female participating in God's kingdom *on earth*. It is a foretaste of the glorious future for men and women in the kingdom.

"The soaring intimacies of love and faith
only make sense to those who participate in
them. Bystanders don't see what all the
commotion is about."

Eugene Peterson[58]

REFERENCES

INTRODUCTION

[1] Dan B. Allender, *Leading with a Limp: Turning Your Struggles into Strengths* (Colorado Springs, Colo.: Waterbrook Press, 2006), 3.

[2] Paul M. Conner, *Celibate Love* (Huntington, Indiana: Our Sunday Visitor, 1979), 171

CHAPTER 1

[1] Gilbert Meilaender, *http://www.firstthings.com/article/2008/09/001-men-and-women-can-we-be-friends-4.*

[2] John R. Scudder and Anne H. Bishop, *Beyond Friendship and Eros: Unrecognized Relationships Between Men and Women* (Albany: State University of New York Press, 2001), 4-5.

[3] Victor Luftig, *Seeing Together: Friendship Between the Sexes in English Writing* (Palo Alto: Stanford University Press, 1993), 1.

[4] Ibid., 1.

[5] Scudder and Bishop, *Beyond Friendship and Eros*, 112.

[6] Luftig, *Seeing Together*, 13.

[7] Ibid., 1

[8] Lillian Calles Barger, *Eve's Revenge: Women and a Spirituality of the Body* (Grand Rapids, MI.: Brazos Press, 2003), 195.

[9] Lewis B. Smedes, *Sex for Christians: The Limits and Liberties of Sexual Living* (Grand Rapids: Eerdmans, 1994), 19.

[10] Rob Bell, *Sex God* (Grand Rapids: Zondervan, 2007), 139.

[11] Mike Mason, *The Mystery of Marriage 20th Anniversary Edition: Meditations on the Miracle* (Portland: Multnomah Books, 2005), 91.

[12] Rob Bell, *Sex God*, 152.

[13] Miroslav Volf, *After Our Likeness: The Church As the Image of the Trinity* (Sacra Doctrina) (Grand Rapids: Eerdmans, 1997), 172.

[14] Louis Colin, *Love One Another* (Westminster, Md: Newman, 1961), 150.

[15] Carmen L. Caltagirone, *Friendship as Sacrament* (New York: Alba House, 1988), 38.

[16] John S. Bonnici, *Person to Person: Friendship and Love in the Life and Theology of Hans Urs Von Balthasar* (New York: Alba House, 1999), 3.

[17] Paul D. O'Callaghan, *Feast of Friendship* (New York: Eighth Day, 2002), 80.

[18] Paul M. Conner, *Celibate Love* (Huntington, Ind.: Our Sunday Visitor, 1979), 171.

[19] Ibid., 96.

[20] Ruth Haley Barton, *Equal to the Task: Men & Women in Partnership* (Downers Grove, Ill.: InterVarsity Press, 1998), 195.

[21] Smedes, *Sex for Christians*, 25.

[22] Gordon J. Hilsman, *Intimate Spirituality: The Catholic Way of Love and Sex* (Lanham: Sheed and Ward, 2007), 3.

[23] Lewis B. Smedes, *Mere Morality: What God Expects from Ordinary People* (Grand Rapids, Mich.: W.B. Eerdmans, 1983), 170.

[24] David M. Carr, *The Erotic Word: Sexuality, Spirituality, and the Bible* (New York: Oxford University Press, 2002), 34.

[25] Elaine Storkey, *The Search for Intimacy* (Grand Rapids: Eerdmans, 1996), 146.

[26] Barton, *Equal to the Task*, 51.

27   Ronald Rolheiser, *Forgotten Among the Lilies: Learning to Love Beyond Our Fears* (New York: Galilee/Doubleday, 2007), 38.

CHAPTER 2

1   Paul J. Wadell, *Becoming Friends: Worship, Justice, and the Practice of Christian Friendship* (Grand Rapids, Mich.: Brazos Press, 2002), 41.

2   Laura Smit, *Loves Me, Loves Me Not: The Ethics of Unrequited Love* (Grand Rapids, Mich.: Baker Academic, 2005), 33.

3   Kathy Werking, *We're Just Good Friends: Women and Men in Nonromantic Relationships* (New York: Guilford Press, 1997), 26.

4   Ibid., 29.

5   Mark Vernon, *The Philosophy of Friendship* (Basingstoke; New York: Palgrave Macmillan, 2005), 49.

6   Frank Tallis, *Love Sick: Love as a Mental Illness* (New York: De Capo Press, 2005), 104.

7   Bruce Brander, *Love That Works: The Art and Science of Giving* (Radnor, Pa.: Templeton Foundation Press, 2004), 99.

8   Helene E. Fisher, *Why We Love: The Nature and Chemistry of Romantic Love* (New York: H. Holt), 2004, 78.

9   Edwin H. Young, *Romancing the Home: How to Have a Marriage That Sizzles* (Nashville, Tenn.: Broadman & Holman Publishers), 1993, 22.

10   Ibid., 23.

11   Ibid., 25.

12   Carolinne White, *Christian Friendship in the Fourth Century* (Cambridge [England]; New York, NY, USA: Cambridge University Press, 1992), 74.

13   Ibid., 158.

14   Ibid., 189.

15   Brian Patrick McGuire, *Friendship & Community: The Monastic Experience, 350-1250* (Cistercian Studies Series No. 95., Kalamazoo, Mich.: Cistercian Publications, 1988), 236.

16   Ibid., 257.

17   Wendy M.Wright, *Bond of Perfection: Jeanne De Chantal & François De Sales* (New enhanced ed. Stella Niagara, N.Y.: DeSales Resource Center, 2001), 116.

18   Richard Godbeer, *The Overflowing of Friendship*, (The John Hopkins University Press, Baltimore, 2009), 56.

19   Sharon Marcus, *Between Women: Friendship, Desire, and Marriage in Victorian England* (Princeton, Princeton University Press, 2007), 57.

20   Liz Carmichael, *Friendship: Interpreting God's Love* (London, T & T Clark International, 2004), 48.

21   Bonnie Fuller, *http://www.huffingtonpost.com/bonnie-fuller/mark-sanford----resignal_b_220942.html.*

22   David Matzko McCarthy, *Love and Sex in the Home: A Theology of the Household* (London: SCM, 2001), 61.

23   Ibid., 64.

24   Fisher, *Why We Love*, 204.

25   Jean Kilbourne, *Can't Buy My Love: How Advertising Changes the Way We Think and Feel* (New York: Touchstone, 1999), 265.

26   James E. Loder, "The Great Sex Charade and the Loss of Intimacy," *Word and World* 21, Winter 2001, 81-87.

27 Christine A. Colón and Bonnie E. Field, *Singled Out: Why Celibacy Must Be Reinvented in Today's Church* (Grand Rapids, Mich: Brazos Press, 2009), 129.

28 Ibid., 131.

29 Loder, "The Great Sex Charade and the Loss of Intimacy."

30 Joseph Epstein, *Friendship: An Exposé* (Boston: Houghton Mifflin Co., 2006), xii-xiii.

31 Lisa Gee, *Friends: Why Men and Women Are from the Same Planet* (New York: Bloomsbury; Distributed to the trade by Holtzbrinck Publishers, 2004), 16.

32 Ibid., 17.

33 Lisa Graham McMinn, *Sexuality and Holy Longing: Embracing Intimacy in a Broken World* (San Francisco: Jossey-Bass, 2004), 77.

34 Tallis, *Love Sick: Love as a Mental Illness*. 286-287.

35 Lauren Winner, *Real Sex: The Naked Truth About Chastity* (Grand Rapids, Mich.: Brazos Press, 2005), 99.

36 Rodney Clapp, *http://www.highlandsstudycenter.org/articles/lousySexLives.php*

37 Philip A. Rolnick, *Person, Grace, and God: (Sacra Doctrina)* (Grand Rapids, Mich.: William B. Eerdmans, 2007), 184, 185.

38 Paul J. Wadell, *Happiness and the Christian Moral Life: An Introduction to Christian Ethics* (Lanham, Md: Rowman & Littlefield Publishers, 2008), 206-207.

39 Kenda Creasy Dean, *Practicing Passion: Youth and the Quest for a Passionate Church* (Grand Rapids, Mich.: Wm. B. Eerdmans, 2004), 137.

CHAPTER 3

1 Sue Edwards, Kelley Matthews and Henry Rogers, *Mixed Ministry: Working Together as Brothers and Sisters in an Oversexed Society* (Grand Rapids, MI: Kregel Publications, 2008), 177.

2 Phyl Newbeck, *Virginia Hasn't Always Been for Lovers: Interracial Marriage Bans and the Case of Richard and Mildred Loving* (Carbondale: Southern Illinois University Press, 2004), 9.

3 Ibid., 25.

4 Ibid., 207.

5 Ibid., 169.

6 Leanne Payne, *Heaven's Calling: A Memoir of One Soul's Steep Ascent* (Grand Rapids, Mich.: Baker Books, 2008), 293.

7 Barbara Ehrenreich and Deirdre English, *For Her Own Good: Two Centuries of the Experts' Advice to Women* (2nd Anchor Books ed. New York: Anchor Books, 2005), 342-343.

8 Martin Luther, in Amy Leonard, *Nails in the Wall: Catholic Nuns in Reformation Germany, Women in Culture and Society*, Amy Leonard, (Chicago: University of Chicago Press, 2005), 1-2.

9 Julie Ingersoll, *Evangelical Christian Women: War Stories in the Gender Battles*, (New York: New York University Press, 2003), 75.

10 Montaigne, quoted in Joan Chittister, *The Friendship of Women: The Hidden Tradition of the Bible* (New York, NY: BlueBridge, 2006), xiv-xv.

11 Victor Luftig, *Seeing Together: Friendship between the Sexes in English Writing from Mill to Woolf* (Stanford, Calif.: Stanford University Press, 1993), 19.

12 Jane Tibbetts Schulenberg, *Forgetful of Their Sex: Female Sanctity and Society*, Ca. 500-1100 (Chicago: University of Chicago Press, 1998), 128-129.

13 Quoted in *Forgetful of Their Sex*, 309.

14 Ibid.

15 Ibid.

16 Jodi Bilinkoff, *Related Lives: Confessors and Their Female Penitents*, 1450-1750 (Ithaca, New York: Cornell, 2005), 19.

17 Schulenberg, *Forgetful of Their Sex*, 289.

18 Ibid., 291.

19 Lisa Gee, *Friends: Why Men and Women Are from the Same Planet* (New York: Bloomsbury, 2004. 2004), 227.

20 Reider Aasgaard, *'My Beloved Brothers and Sisters!': Christian Siblingship in Paul* (New York: T&T Clark International, 2004), 73.

21 Schulenberg, *Forgetful of Their Sex*, 284.

22 Ibid., 304-305.

23 Leonore Davidoff, "The Sibling Relationship and Sibling Incest in Historical Context," in *Sibling Relationships*, ed. Prophecy Coles (London: H. Karnac LTD., 2006), 24.

24 Quoted in Stephen P. Bank and Michael D. Kahn, *The Sibling Bond* (New York: Basic Books, 1982), 162.

25 Gee, *Friends*, 28.26

26 Ibid., 35.

27 Ibid., 18.

28 Alice P. Matthews and M. Gay Hubbard, *Marriage Made in Eden: A Pre-Modern Perspective for a Post-Christian World* (Grand Rapids, Mich.: Baker Books, 2004), 207.

29 Joseph H. Hellerman, *The Ancient Church as Family* (Minneapolis, MN: Fortress Press, 2001), 37.

30 Anthony J. Gittins, "In Search of Goodenough Families," in *Mutuality Matters: Family, Faith, and Just Love*, ed. by Herbert Anderson, Edward Foley, Bonnie Miller-McLemore, and Robert Schreiter (Lanham, Md.: Rowman & Littlefield Publishers, 2004), 175.

31 Lilian Calles Barger, *Eve's Revenge: Women and a Spirituality of the Body* (Grand Rapids, MI: Brazos Press, 2003), 117.

32 Daniel Taylor, T*ell Me a Story: The Life-Shaping Power of Our Stories* (St. Paul, MN: Bog Walk Press, 2001), 7.

33 Laura A. Smit, *Loves Me, Loves Me Not: The Ethics of Unrequited Love* (Grand Rapids, MI: Baker Academic, 2005), 70.

34 Schulenburg, *Forgetful of Their Sex*, 307.

35 Wendy M. Wright, *Bond of Perfection: Jeanne De Chantal & François De Sales* (New enhanced ed. Stella Niagara, N.Y.: DeSales Resource Center, 2001), 17, 19.

36 Schulenburg, *Forgetful of Their Sex*, 307.

37 Bilinkoff, *Related Lives*, 95.

38 Ibid., 18.

39 Schulenburg, *Forgetful of Their Sex*, 324-325.

40 Wright, *Bond of Perfection*, 29.

41 Schulenburg, *Forgetful of Their Sex*, 327.

42 Ibid., 336.

43 Ibid., 310.

44 Ibid., 323.

45 Ibid., 338.

46 Ibid., 339.

47 Wendy M. Wright, "The Spiritual Friendships of Francis de Sales and Jane de Chantal," http://www4.desales.edu/SCFC/Studies/WW-SpirFriendship.pdf.

48 Kathleen Norris, *The Cloister Walk* (New York: Riverhead Books, 1996), 117.

49 Wright, *Bond of Perfection* 55.

⁵⁰ Terrence A. McGoldrick, *The Sweet and Gentle Struggle: Francis de Sales and the Necessity of Spiritual Friendship* (Lanham: University Press of America, 1996), 142.

⁵¹ Wright, *Bond of Perfection*, 58.

⁵² Carole Hallundbaek, *Saints in Love: The Forgotten Loves between Holy Women and Men and How They Can Make Our Relationships Divine* (New York: Crossroad, 2007), 167.

⁵³ Ibid., 173.

⁵⁴ Wendy M. Wright and Joseph F. Power, Francis De Sales, *Jane De Chantal: Letters of Spiritual Direction* (Classics of Western Spirituality. New York: Paulist Press, 1988), 4-5.

⁵⁵ Wright, *Bond of Perfection*, 150.

⁵⁶ Schulenburg, *Forgetful of Their Sex*, 334.

⁵⁷ Brian Patrick McGuire, *Friendship & Community: The Monastic Experience, 350-1250* (Cistercian Studies Series No. 95. Kalamazoo, Mich.: Cistercian Publications, 1988), 108.

⁵⁸ Ibid.

⁵⁹ Dan B. Allender, *Leading with a Limp: Turning Your Struggles into Strengths* (Colorado Springs, Colorado: Waterbrook Press, 2006), 121.

⁶⁰ Cited in Hallundbaek, *Saints in Love*, 168.

⁶¹ Wright, and Power, *Francis De Sales, Jane De Chantal : Letters of Spiritual Direction*, 3.

CHAPTER 4

¹ Robert E. Webber, *The Divine Embrace: Recovering the Passionate Spiritual Life* (Grand Rapids: Baker Books, 2006), 18.

² Kevin J. Vanhoozer, *The Drama of Doctrine: A Canonical-Linguistic Approach To Christian Theology* (Louisville: Westminster John Knox, 2005), 331.

³ Scot McKnight, *The Blue Parakeet: Rethinking How You Read the Bible* (Grand Rapids: Zondervan, 2008), 71.

⁴ Paul J. Wadell, *Happiness and the Christian Moral Life: An Introduction to Christian Ethics* (Lanham, Md.: Rowman & Littlefield Publishers, 2008), 144.

⁵ James H. Olthuis, "Be(com)ing: Humankind as Gift and Call," *Philosophia Reformata* 58, 1993, 153-172.

⁶ Rosemary Rader, *Breaking Boundaries: Male/Female Friendship in Early Christian Communities* (New York: Paulist Press, 1983), 34.

⁷ Wendy M. Wright, "*Reflections on Spiritual Friendship between Men and Women*," Weavings, July 1987, 13-23.

⁸ L. William Countryman, *Dirt, Greed, and Sex: Sexual Ethics in the New Testament and Their Implications for Today* (Rev. ed. Minneapolis: Fortress Press, 2007), 216.

⁹ Lisa Graham McMinn, *Sexuality and Holy Longing: Embracing Intimacy in a Broken World* (San Francisco: Jossey-Bass, 2004), 138.

¹⁰ Kenda Creasy Dean, *Practicing Passion: Youth and the Quest for a Passionate Church* (Grand Rapids, Mich.: Eerdmans Pub., 2004), 68.

¹¹ Dennis W. Hiebert, "Toward Adult Cross-Sex Friendship," *Journal of Psychology and Theology* 24, no. No. 4 (1996): 271-83.

¹² Ibid.

¹³ Stanley J. Grenz, *Sexual Ethics: A Biblical Perspective* (Dallas: Word Pub., 1990), 8.

¹⁴ James H. Olthuis, *I Pledge You My Troth: A Christian View of Marriage, Family, Friendship* (New York: Harper & Row, 1975), 115.

¹⁵ Marva J. Dawn, *In the Beginning, God: Creation, Culture, and the Spiritual Life* (Downers Grove, Ill.: IVP Books, 2009), 84.

16 Paul J. Wadell, *Becoming Friends: Worship, Justice, and the Practice of Christian Friendship* (Grand Rapids: Brazos, 2002), 81.

17 McKnight, *The Blue Parakeet*, 168.

18 Ibid., 179-183.

19 David Bentley Hart, *The Beauty of the Infinite: The Aesthetics of Christian Truth* (Grand Rapids, Mich.: W.B. Eerdmans, 2003), 21.

20 Kristina LaCelle-Peterson, *Liberating Tradition: Women's Identity and Vocation in Christian Perspective* (Grand Rapids, Mich.: Baker Academic, 2008), 226.

21 Ibid., 210.

22 Stanley J. Grenz, *The Social God and the Relational Self* (Louisville: Westminster John Knox, 2001), 303.

23 Wadell, *Becoming Friends*, 91.

24 Christine A. Colón and Bonnie E. Field, *Singled Out: Why Celibacy Must Be Reinvented in Today's Church* (Grand Rapids, Mich.: Brazos Press, 2009), 158.

25 Paul O'Callaghan, *The Feast of Friendship* (Wichita: Eighth Day Press, 2002), 136.

26 Lilian Calles Barger, *Chasing Sophia: Reclaiming the Lost Wisdom of Jesus* (San Francisco: Jossey-Bass, 2007), 97.

27 Ralph Waldo Emerson and Edward Waldo Emerson, *The Complete Works of Ralph Waldo Emerson* (Cambridge: Riverside Press, 1903), 209.

28 Ibid., 201.

29 Caroline J. Simon, *The Disciplined Heart: Love, Destiny, and Imagination* (Grand Rapids, Mich.: W.B. Eerdmans Pub., 1997), 88.

30 Wendy M. Wright, *Sacred Dwelling: An Everyday Family Spiritualilty* (Boston, MA: Pauline Books & Media, 2007), 95.

31 Kathleen A. Bogle, *Hooking Up: Sex, Dating, and Relationships on Campus* (New York: New York University Press, 2008), 125.

32 Gary R. Brooks, *The Centerfold Syndrome: How Men Can Overcome Objectification and Achieve Intimacy with Women* (San Francisco: Jossey-Bass Publishers, 1995), 23.

33 Ibid., 31.

34 Douglas E. Rosenau and Michael R. Sytsma, "A Theology of Sexual Intimacy: Insights into the Creator," *Journal of Psychology and Christianity* Vol. 23, No. 3 (2004): 261-270.

35 David G. Benner, *Sacred Companions: The Gift of Spiritual Friendship & Direction* (Downers Grove, Ill.: InterVarsity Press, 2002), 187..

36 Carmen Renee Berry, *The Unauthorized Guide to Sex and the Church* (Nashville, Tenn.: W Pub. Group, 2005), 15.

37 Judith K. Balswick, and Jack O. Balswick, *Authentic Human Sexuality: An Integrated Christian Approach* (Downers Grove, Ill.: InterVarsity Press, 1999), 42.

38 Christine Gudorf, "The Graceful Pleasures: Why Sex is Good for Marriage," in *Human Sexuality in the Catholic Tradition*, ed. Kieran Scott and Harold Daly Horell (Lanham, Md.: Rowman & Littlefield Publishers, 2007), 136.

39 Elizabeth A. Dreyer, *Earth Crammed with Heaven: A Spirituality of Everyday Life* (New York: Paulist Press, 1994), 120.

40 Elizabeth A. Dreyer, *Passionate Spirituality: Hildegard of Bingen and Hadewijch of Brabant* (Mahwah, N.J.: Paulist Press, 2005), 44.

41 Lewis B. Smedes, *Sex for Christians: The Limits and Liberties of Sexual Living* (Rev. ed. Grand Rapids, Mich.: W.B. Eerdmans, 1994), 3.

42 Gudorf, "The Graceful Pleasures," 124-125.

[43] Ibid., 131.

[44] Rob Bell, *Sex God: Exploring the Endless Connections between Sexuality and Spirituality* (Grand Rapids, Mich.: Zondervan, 2007), 138-139.

[45] Dan B. Allender, and Tremper Longman, *The Intimate Mystery: Creating Strength and Beauty in Your Marriage* (Downers Grove, Ill.: InterVarsity Press, 2005), 82.

[46] Alice P. Matthews and M. Gay Hubbard, *Marriage Made in Eden: A Pre-Modern Perspective for a Post-Christian World* (Grand Rapids, Mich.: Baker Books, 2004), 201.

[47] Edith M. Humphrey, *Ecstasy and Intimacy: When the Holy Spirit Meets the Human Spirit* (Grand Rapids: Wm. B. Eerdmans, 2006), 92.

[48] Dean, *Practicing Passion*, 89.

[49] Gordon J. Hilsman, *Intimate Spirituality: The Catholic Way of Love and Sex* (Lanham, Md.: Rowman & Littlefield Publishers, 2007), 131.

[50] Elizabeth A. Dreyer, *Making Sense of God: A Woman's Perspective* (Cincinnati, OH: St. Anthony Messenger Press, 2008), 69,70.

[51] David Bentley Hart, *The Beauty of the Infinite: The Aesthetics of Christian Truth* (Grand Rapids, Mich.: W.B. Eerdmans, 2003), 20.

[52] John Navone, *Toward a Theology of Beauty* (Collegeville, Mn.,: The Liturgical Press, 1996), 18.

[53] Ibid., 137.

[54] Sally B. Purvis, "A Common Love: Christian Feminist Ethics and Family," in *Doing Right and Being Good: Catholic and Protestant Readings in Christian Ethics*, ed. David Oki Ahearn, and Peter R. Gathje (Collegeville, Minn.: Liturgical Press, 2005), 130.

[55] Ibid., 137.

[56] Marva J. Dawn, *The Sense of the Call: A Sabbath Way of Life for Those who Serve God, the Church, and the World* (Grand Rapids, MI: Wm. B. Eerdmans Publishing, 2006), 195.

[57] Joan Chittister, *The Friendship of Women: The Hidden Tradition of the Bible* (New York, NY: BlueBridge, 2006), x.

[58] Carmen Caltagirone, *Friendship as Sacrament* (New York: Alba House, 1988), 36, 37.

[59] Simon, *The Disciplined Heart*. 99.

[60] Vincent J. Genovesi, *In Pursuit of Love: Catholic Morality and Human Sexuality* (2nd ed. Collegeville, Minn.: Liturgical Press, 1996), 132.

[61] Ibid., 134.

[62] Ibid., 133-134.

[63] Ruth Hudson, *http://infidelitynewsandviews.blogspot.com/2009/06/sanford-affair-infidelity-experts.html*.

[64] Irene S. Levine, *Best Friends Forever: Surviving a Breakup with Your Best Friend* (New York: The Overlook Press, 2009), 33.

[65] Donna Downes, "Confused Ministry Roles—Theirs or Mine?," in *Frontline Women: Negotiating Crosscultural Issues in Ministry*, ed. Marguerite G. Kraft. Pasadena, (Calif.: William Carey Library, 2003), 125-126.

[66] Sandy Sheehy, *Connecting: The Enduring Power of Female Friendship* (New York: William Morrow, 2000), 9.

[67] Sharon Marcus, *Between Women: Friendship, Desire, and Marriage in Victorian England* (Princeton: Princeton University Press, 2007), 66-67.

[68] Richard Godbeer, *The Overflowing of Friendship: Love between Men and the Creation of the American Republic* (Baltimore: Johns Hopkins University Press, 2009), 85.

[69] Grenz, *The Social God and the Relational Self*. 302

[70] Paul O'Callaghan, *The Feast of Friendship* (Wichita: Eighth Day Press, 2002), 136.

[71]   James R. Payton, *Light from the Christian East: An Introduction to the Orthodox Tradition* (Downers Grove, Ill.: IVP Academic, 2007). 85.

[72]   Ronald Rolheiser, *Forgotten among the Lilies: Learning to Live Beyond Our Fears* (New York: Galilee/Doubleday, 2005), 73.

[73]   Ruth Haley Barton, *Equal to the Task: Men & Women in Partnership* (Downers Grove, Ill.: InterVarsity Press, 1998), 199.

[74]   Hiebert, "Toward Adult Cross-Sex Friendship." 271-283.

[75]   Douglas Rosenau and Michael Todd Wilson, *Soul Virgins: Redefining Single Sexuality* (Grand Rapids, Mich.: Baker Books, 2006), 37.

CHAPTER 5

[1]   David M. Carr, *The Erotic Word: Sexuality, Spirituality, and the Bible* (New York: Oxford University Press, USA, 2002), 13.

[2]   Erwin Lutzer and Rebecca Lutzer, *Jesus, Lover of a Woman's Soul* (Carol Stream: Tyndale House Publishers, 2006), 15.

[3]   Susan Ackerman, *When Heroes Love: The Ambiguity of Eros in the Stories of Gilgamesh and David* (Irvington: Columbia University Press, 2005), 176.

[4]   Ibid., 176.

[5]   Ibid., 176-177.

[6]   Ibid., 177.

[7]   Robert Brain, *Friends and Lovers* (New York: Basic Books, 1976), 28,

[8]   Ibid., 30.

[9]   Ibid., 33.

[10]   Paul D. O'Callaghan, *The Feast of Friendship* (Wichita, KS: Eighth Day Press, 2002), 46.

[11]   Richard Godbeer, *The Overflowing of Friendship: Love between Men and the Creation of the American Republic* (Baltimore: Johns Hopkins University Press, 2009), 6-7.

[12]   Brian Patrick McGuire, *Friendship & Community: The Monastic Experience*, 350-1250 (Cistercian Studies Series No. 95. Kalamazoo, Mich.: Cistercian Publications, 1988), 391.

[13]   Gerald Vann, *To Heaven with Diana!* (Lincoln, NE: Dominican Nuns of the Perpetual Rosary, 2006, Reprint), 26.

[14]   Jodi Bilinkoff, *Related Lives: Confessors and Their Female Penitents*, 1450-1750 (Ithaca, N.Y.: Cornell University Press, 2005), 82.

[15]   Sandy Sheehy, *Connecting: The Enduring Power of Female Friendship* (New York: William Morrow, 2000), 9-10.

[16]   Joseph Epstein, *Friendship: An Expose* (New York: Mariner Books, 2007), 57.

[17]   Judith A. Kates and Gail Twersky Reimer, *Reading Ruth: Contemporary Women Reclaim a Sacred Story* (New York: Random House, 1994), 31.

[18]   Dan B. Allender, *Leading with a Limp: Turning Your Struggles into Strengths* (Colorado Springs: WaterBrook Press, 2006), 115.

[19]   Carr, *The Erotic Word*, 164, 165.

[20]   Laura A. Smit, *Loves Me, Love Me Not: The Ethics of Unrequited Love* (Grand Rapids: Baker Publishing, 2005), 69-70.

[21]   Elisabeth Moltmann-Wendel, *Rediscovering Friendship: Awakening to the Power and Promise of Women's Friendships* (Minneapolis: Augsburg Fortress Publishers, 2001), 70.

[22]   Wendy M. Wright, "Reflections on Spiritual Friendship," *Weavings* 2, no. 4 (1987): 15.

[23]   Paul J. Wadell, *Happiness and the Christian Moral Life: An Introduction to Christian Ethics* (Lanham: Rowman & Littlefield Publishers, Inc., 2007), 199.

24 Scott F. Spencer, *Dancing Girls, Loose Ladies, and Women of the Cloth: The Women In Jesus' Life* (New York: Continuum International Publishing Group, 2004), 98, 99.
25 Wright, "Reflections on Spiritual Friendship."
26 Elizabeth A. Dreyer, *Passionate Spirituality: Hildegard of Bingen and Hadewijch of Brabant* (Mahwah, N.J.: Paulist Press, 2005), 141.
27 Sharon H. Ringe, *Wisdom's Friends: Community and Christology in the Fourth Gospel* (Louisville: Westiminster John Knox Press, 1999), 76.
28 Moltmann-Wendel, *Rediscovering Friendship*, 72.
29 Andy Crouch, *Culture Making: Recovering Our Creative Calling* (Downers Grove, Ill.: IVP Books, 2008), 136, 138.
30 L. William Countryman, *Love, Human and Divine: Reflections on Love, Sexuality, and Friendship* (Harrisburg, Pa.: Morehouse Pub., 2005), 39.
31 Jürgen Moltmann, *The Spirit of Life: A Universal Affirmation* (Minneapolis: Fortress Press, 1992), 119.
32 Jane Schaberg, *Resurrection of Mary Magdalene: Legends, Apocrypha, and the Christian Testament* (New York: Continuum International Publishing Group, 2004), 330.
33 Ibid., 330.
34 Celia A. Hahn, *Sexual Paradox: Creative Tensions in Our Lives and in Our Congregations* (New York: Pilgrim Press, 1991), 166.
35 Darrel L. Bock, *Breaking the Da Vinci Code: Answers to the Questions Everyone's Asking* (New York: Thomas Nelson, 2006), 18.
36 Frances T. Gench, *Encounters with Jesus: Studies in the Gospel of John* (Louisville: Westminster John Knox Press, 2007), 132.
37 Carr, *The Erotic Word*, 166.
38 Ibid.
39 Scott F. Spencer, *Dancing Girls, Loose Ladies, and Women of the Cloth: The Women In Jesus' Life* (New York: Continuum International Publishing Group, 2004), 99.
40 Moltmann-Wendel, Elisabeth, *The Women Around Jesus* (New York: The Crossroad Publishing Company, 1982), 71.
41 Carr, *The Erotic Word*, 173.
42 Andy Rooney, *http://www.cbsnews.com/stories/2002/03/29/60minutes/main504971.shtml.*
43 James B. Nelson and Sandra P. Longfellow, *Sexuality and the Sacred: Sources for Theological Reflection* (Louisville, Ky.: Westminster/John Knox Press, 1994), 101, 97.
44 Janice G. Raymond, *A Passion for Friends: Toward a Philosophy of Female Affection* (Boston: Beacon Press, 1986), 227.
45 bell hooks, *Communion: The Female Search for Love* (New York: W. Morrow, 2002), 210.
46 Catherine Mowry LaCugna, *God for Us: The Trinity and Christian Life* (San Francisco: HarperSanFrancisco, 1991), 407.
47 C.S. Lewis, *The Four Loves* (New York: Hartcourt Brace Jovanich, 1991), 169
48 Parker J. Palmer, *To Know as We Are Known: Education as a Spiritual Journey* (San Francisco: HarperCollins, 1993), 8.
49 LaCugna, *God for Us*, 294.

CHAPTER 6

1 Lilian Barger, *Eve's Revenge: Women and a Spirituality of the Body* (Grand Rapids: Brazos, 2003), 117.

2   Richard Beck, *http://experimentaltheology.blogspot.com/2009/10/purity-and-defilement-part-14-disgust.html*.
3   Vincent J. Genovesi, *In Pursuit of Love: Catholic Morality and Human Sexuality* (2nd ed. Collegeville, Minn.: Liturgical Press, 1996), 126.
4   Raymond J. Lawrence, *Sexual Liberation: The Scandal of Christendom* (Westport, Conn.: Praeger Publishers, 2007), 8.
5   Rosemary Rader, *Breaking Boundaries: Male/Female Friendship in Early Christian Communities* (New York: Paulist Press, 1983), 4.
6   Jürgen Moltmann and Elisabeth Moltmann-Wendel, *Passion for God: Theology in Two Voices* (Louisville, Ky.: Westminster John Knox Press, 2003), 41.
7   Kenneth E. Bailey, *Jesus through Middle Eastern Eyes: Cultural Studies in the Gospels* (Downers Grove, Ill.: IVP Academic, 2008), 193.
8   Ibid., 190.
9   "Rethinking Jewish Sexual Ethics," Judith Plaskow, Kathleen M. Sands, *God Forbid: Religion and Sex in American Public Life* (New York: Oxford University Press, 2000), 28.
10 Lawrence, *Sexual Liberation*, 9.
11 Rodney Clapp, *Tortured Wonders: Christian Spirituality for People, Not Angels* (Grand Rapids, Mich.: Brazos Press, 2004), 194.
12 Barbara E. Reid, *Choosing the Better Part?: Women in the Gospel of Luke* (Collegeville, Minn.: Liturgical Press, 1996), 110.
13 Nancy Tuana, *The Less Noble Sex: Scientific, Religions, and Philosophical Conceptions of Woman's Nature* (Bloomington: Indiana University Press, 1993), 155-156.
14 Ibid. 156.
15 Bailey, *Jesus through Middle Eastern Eyes*, 248.
16 Brian Thorne, *Infinitely Beloved: The Challenge of Divine Intimacy*, (London: Darton Longman & Todd Ltd, 2003), 64.
17 Andrew M. Greeley, *Jesus: A Meditation on His Stories and His Relationships with Women* (New York: Forge Books, 2008), 94.
18 Barger, *Eve's Revenge*, 159.
19 Ibid.
20 Kristina LaCelle-Peterson, *Liberating Tradition: Women's Identity and Vocation in Christian Perspective* (Grand Rapids, Mich.: Baker Academic, 2008), 103.
21 Carrie A. Miles, *The Redemption of Love: Rescuing Marriage and Sexuality from the Economics of a Fallen World* (Grand Rapids, Mich.: Brazos Press, 2006), 65.
22 Wendy Corbin Reuschling, *Reviving Evangelical Ethics: The Promises and Pitfalls of Classic Models of Morality* (Grand Rapids, Mich.: Brazos Press, 2008), 165.
23 F. Scott Spencer, *Dancing Girls, Loose Ladies, and Women of the Cloth: The Women in Jesus' Life* (New York: Continuum, 2004), 115.
24 Ibid., 116.
25 Sue Edwards and Kelley Mathews and Henry J. Rogers, *Mixed Ministry: Working Together as Brothers and Sisters in an Oversexed Society* (Grand Rapids: Kregal, 2008), 152.
26 Paul J. Wadell, *Happiness and the Christian Moral Life: An Introduction to Christian Ethics* (Lanham, Md.: Rowman & Littlefield Publishers, 2008), 209.
27 Mark Vernon, *The Philosophy of Friendship* (New York: Palgrave Macmillan, 2005), 134.
28 Thorne, *Infinitely Beloved*, 64-65.
29 John S. Grabowski, *Sex and Virtue: An Introduction to Sexual Ethics* (Catholic University of America Press, 2003), 84.
30 Thorne, *Infinitely Beloved*, 65.

[31] *http://blog.pastors.com/2007/04/30/saddleback-staff-ten-commandments/*

[32] Douglas Rosenau and Michael Todd Wilson, *Soul Virgins: Redefining Single Sexuality* (Grand Rapids, Mich.: Baker Books, 2006), 219.

[33] Reuschling, *Reviving Evangelical Ethics*, 123.

[34] Joseph C. Aldrich, *Lifestyle Evangelism: Crossing Traditional Boundaries to Reach the Unbelieving World*, (Portland, OR: Multnomah Press, 1981), 55.

[35] Dan Russ, *Flesh-and-Blood Jesus: Learning to Be Fully Human from the Son of Man* (Grand Rapids, MI: Baker Books, 2008), 102.

[36] Jürgen Moltmann, *The Spirit of Life: A Universal Affirmation* (Minneapolis: Fortress Press, 1992), 115.

[37] Dan B. Allender and Tremper Longman, *Intimate Allies: Rediscovering God's Design for Marriage and Becoming Soul Mates for Life* (Wheaton, Ill.: Tyndale House Publishers, 1995), 92.

[38] Wendy M. Wright, *Sacred Dwelling: An Everyday Family Spirituality* (Boston, MA: Pauline Books & Media, 2007), 95.

[39] Philip A. Rolnick, *Person, Grace, and God* (Grand Rapids, Mich.: William B. Eerdmans, 2007), 253.

[40] LaCelle-Peterson, *Liberating Tradition*, 86.

[41] John R. Scudder and Anne H. Bishop, *Beyond Friendship and Eros: Unrecognized Relationships between Men and Women* (Albany: State University of New York Press, 2001), 114.

[42] Alvin J. Schmidt, *Veiled and Silenced: How Culture Shaped Sexist Theology* (Macon, Ga.: Mercer University Press, 1989), 131.

[43] Grabowski, *Sex and Virtue*, 85.

[44] Paul J. Wadell, *Friendship and the Moral Life* (Notre Dame, Ind.: University of Notre Dame Press, 1989), 163.

[45] Vincent J. Genovesi, *In Pursuit of Love: Catholic Morality and Human Sexuality* (2nd ed. Collegeville, Minn.: Liturgical Press, 1996), 135.

[46] Scudder and Bishop, *Beyond Friendship and Eros*, 112.

[47] Ibid., 184-185.

[48] Genovesi, *In Pursuit of Love*, 136.

[49] Ronald Rolheiser, *Forgotten Among the Lilies: Learning to Live Beyond Our Fears* (New York: Galilee/Doubleday, 2005), 38.

[50] Ibid., 52, 70.

[51] Grabowski, *Sex and Virtue*, 87.

[52] Barger, *Eve's Revenge*, 151.

[53] Ibid., 134.

[54] Grabowski, *Sex and Virtue*, 166.

[55] Kenda Creasy Dean, *Practicing Passion: Youth and the Quest for a Passionate Church* (Grand Rapids, Mich.: Eerdmans Pub., 2004), 118.

[56] Arthur O. Roberts and Robin Shepard, *Messengers of God: The Sensuous Side of Spirituality* (2nd ed. Newburg, OR: Barclay, 2006), 173.

[57] Barger, *Eve's Revenge*, 116.

[58] James H. Olthuis, *I Pledge You My Troth: A Christian View of Marriage, Family, Friendship* (New York: Harper & Row, 1975), 115.

[59] Dean, *Practicing Passion*, 132.

[60] Ibid., 132.

[61] Genovesi, *In Pursuit of Love*, 140.

[62] Roberts and Shepard, *Messengers of God*, 173.

[63] Ruth Haley Barton, *Equal to the Task: Men & Women in Partnership* (Downers Grove, Ill.: InterVarsity Press, 1998), 194.

CHAPTER 7

[1] Goscelin, and Monika Otter, *Goscelin of St. Bertin: The Book of Encouragement and Consolation* (Rochester, NY: D.S. Brewer, 2004), 148.

[2] C. S. Lewis, *The Four Loves* (New York,: Harcourt, 1960), 80.

[3] Eugene H. Peterson and Jim Lyster and John Sharon, and Peter Santucci, *Subversive Spirituality* (Grand Rapids, Mich.: W.B. Eerdmans, 1997. 241.

[4] Liz Carmichael, *Friendship: Interpreting Christian Love* (New York: T & T Clark International, 2004), 198.

[5] Rebecca G. Adams and Graham Allan, *Placing Friendship in Context* (Cambridge: Cambridge University Press, 1998), 2.

[6] Laura A. Smit, *Loves Me, Loves Me Not: The Ethics of Unrequited Love* (Grand Rapids, Mich.: Baker Academic, 2005), 64-65.

[7] Kevin J. Vanhoozer, *The Drama of Doctrine: A Canonical-Linguistic Approach to Christian Theology* (Louisville: Westminster John Knox Press, 2005), 397.

[8] Miroslav Volf, *Exclusion and Embrace: A Theological Exploration of Identity, Otherness, and Reconciliation* (Nashville: Abingdon Press, 1996), 182.

[9] Madeleine L'Engle, and Giotto, *The Glorious Impossible* (New York: Simon and Schuster Books for Young Readers, 1990).

[10] David Matzko McCarthy, *The Good Life: Genuine Christianity for the Middle Class* (Grand Rapids, Mich.: Brazos Press, 2004), 35.

[11] Brian J. Walsh and Steven Bouma-Prediger, "With and Without Boundaries," in *The Hermeneutics of Charity: Interpretation, Selfhood, and Postmodern Faith* ed. James K. A. Smith and Henry Isaac Venema, and James H. Olthuis (Grand Rapids, Mich.: Brazos Press, 2004), 235.

[12] Dan B. Allender, *The Wounded Heart* (Rev. ed. Colorado Springs, Colo.: NavPress, 1995), 195.

[13] Paul J Wadell, *Happiness and the Christian Moral Life: An Introduction to Christian Ethics* (Lanham, Md.: Rowman & Littlefield Publishers, 2008), 41.

[14] McCarthy, *The Good Life*, 35, 37.

[15] Eugene H. Peterson, *Five Smooth Stones for Pastoral Work* (Grand Rapids, Mich.: W.B. Eerdmans, 1992), 60.

[16] Ibid., 53.

[17] James H. Olthuis, "Face-to-Face," in *The Hermeneutics of Charity: Interpretation, Selfhood, and Postmodern Faith* ed. James K. A. Smith and Henry Isaac Venema, and James H. Olthuis (Grand Rapids, Mich.: Brazos Press, 2004), 152.

[18] Wadell, *Happiness and the Christian Moral Life*, 154.

[19] Ibid.

[20] Paul J. Wadell, *Becoming Friends: Worship, Justice, and the Practice of Christian Friendship* (Grand Rapids, Mich.: Brazos Press, 2002), 165.

[21] Jane Tibbets Schulenburg, *Forgetful of Their Sex* (Chicago: University of Chicago Press, 1998), 311.

[22] David Bentley Hart, *The Beauty of the Infinite: The Aesthetics of Christian Truth* (Grand Rapids, Mich.: W.B. Eerdmans, 2003), 20.

[23] Christine Gudorf, "A New Moral Discourse on Sexuality," in Kieran Scott and Harold Daly Horell (*Human Sexuality in the Catholic Tradition*. Lanham, Md.: Rowman & Littlefield Publishers, 2007), 65.

24 Hart, *The Beauty of the Infinite*, 253.

25 Ibid., 255.

26 Norman Wirzba, *Living the Sabbath: Discovering the Rhythms of Rest and Delight* (Grand Rapids, Mich.: Brazos Press, 2006), 53, 62.

27 Wirzba, *Living the Sabbath*, 59.

28 Wadell, *Happiness and the Christian Moral Life*, 206.

29 Ruth Haley Barton, *Equal to the Task: Men & Women in Partnership* (Downers Grove, Ill.: InterVarsity Press, 1998), 61.

30 Christine A. Colón and Bonnie E. Field, *Singled Out: Why Celibacy Must Be Reinvented in Today's Church* (Grand Rapids, Mich.: Brazos Press, 2009). 95.

31 Andy Crouch, *Culture Making: Recovering Our Creative Calling* (Downers Grove, Ill.: IVP Books, 2008), 48.

32 Lisa Gee, *Friends: Why Men and Women Are from the Same Planet* (New York: Bloomsbury, 2004), 42.

33 William K. Rawlins, *The Compass of Friendship: Narratives, Identities, and Dialogues* (Los Angeles, Calif.: Sage Publications, 2009), 125.

34 Luci Taylor, *http://www.dailymail.co.uk/femail/article-1210077/Why-women-need-male-friends-stop-sex-getting-way.html*.

35 David G. Benner, *Sacred Companions: The Gift of Spiritual Friendship & Direction* (Downers Grove, Ill.: InterVarsity Press, 2002), 187.

36 Dan B. Allender, *Leading with a Limp: Turning Your Struggles into Strengths* (Colorado Springs, Colo.: Waterbrook Press, 2006), 85.

37 Elaine Storkey, *The Search for Intimacy* (Grand Rapids, Mich.: William B. Eerdmans Pub., 1996), 140.

38 David K. Naugle, *Reordered Love, Reordered Lives: Learning the Deep Meaning of Happiness* (Grand Rapids, Mich.: William B. Eerdmans Pub., 2008), 42.

39 Christine E. Gudorf, *Body, Sex, and Pleasure: Reconstructing Christian Sexual Ethics* (Cleveland, Ohio: Pilgrim Press, 1994), 85, 86.

40 Wirzba, *Living the Sabbath*, 59.

41 Gigi M. Durham, *The Lolita Effect: The Media Sexualization of Young Girls and What We Can Do About It* (Woodstock, New York: Overlook, 2008), 108.

42 Lisa Graham McMinn, *Sexuality and Holy Longing: Embracing Intimacy in a Broken World* (San Francisco: Jossey-Bass, 2004), 165.

43 Wadell, *Happiness and the Christian Moral Life*, 179-180.

44 Stuart L. Brown and Christopher C. Vaughan, *Play: How It Shapes the Brain, Opens the Imagination, and Invigorates the Soul* (New York: Avery, 2009), 17.

45 Ibid., 162.

46 Kenda Creasy Dean, *Practicing Passion: Youth and the Quest for a Passionate Church* (Grand Rapids, Mich.: Eerdmans Pub., 2004), 200.

47 Lewis B. Smedes, *Mere Morality: What God Expects from Ordinary People* (Grand Rapids, Mich.: W.B. Eerdmans Pub. Co., 1983), 169.

48 Mark Buchanan, *The Rest of God: Restoring Your Soul by Restoring Sabbath* (Nashville, Tenn.: W Pub. Group, 2006), 139.

49 Vanhoozer, *The Drama of Doctrine*, 387.

50 Dean, *Practicing Passion*, 209.

51 Gareth Weldon Icenogle, *Biblical Foundations for Small Group Ministry: An Integrative Approach* (Downers Grove, Ill.: InterVarsity Press, 1994), 57.

52 Wadell, *Becoming Friends: Worship, Justice, and the Practice of Christian Friendship* (Grand Rapids, Mich.: Brazos Press, 2002), 85.

53 Scot McKnight, *The Blue Parakeet: Rethinking How You Read the Bible* (Grand Rapids, Mich.: Zondervan, 2008), 103.

54 Irene Stiver, "The Meaning of 'Dependency' in *Male-Female Relationships*." (ed.Wellesley Centers for Women. Wellesley, MA), 1984.

55 David S. Cunningham, "*Participation as a Trinitarian Virtue*." Toronto Journal of Theology 14, no. 1 (1998): 7-25.

56 Edith M. Humphrey, *Ecstasy and Intimacy: When the Holy Spirit Meets the Human Spirit* (Grand Rapids, Mich.: W.B. Eerdmans Pub. Co., 2006), 192.

57 Samuel Shem and Janet L. Surrey, *We Have to Talk: Healing Dialogues between Women and Men* (New York, NY: Basic Books, 1998), 50.

58 Peterson, *Five Smooth Stones for Pastoral Work*, 69.

CPSIA information can be obtained
at www.ICGtesting.com
Printed in the USA
BVHW031735120620
581249BV00004B/100